A TREASURY OF GREAT ADIRONDACK STORIES

A TREASURY OF
GREAT ADIRONDACK STORIES

as retold by

John Vinton

**Illustrations by Larry Miller
incorporating images from
Seneca Ray Stoddard**

NORTH COUNTRY BOOKS
Utica, New York

A Treasury of
Great Adirondack Stories

Copyright © 1991
by
John Vinton

ISBN 0-932052-35-5

FIRST PAPERBACK EDITION 1991
SECOND PAPERBACK EDITION 2001

Library of Congress Cataloging-in-Publication Data

Vinton, John
    A treasury of great Adirondack stories / as told by John Vinton ;
illustrations by Larry Miller incorporating images from Seneca Ray
Stoddard ; introduction by George D. Davis.
      p.   cm.
Includes bibliographical references and indexes.
ISBN 0-932052-34-7. - ISBN 0-932052-35-5 (pbk.)
1. Adirondack Mountains Region (N.Y.) — Fiction. 2. Tales – New
York (State) — Adirondack Mountains Region.   I. Title.
PS3572.1577T74   1991
813'.54—dc20   91-29637
                                               CIP

Published by
North Country Books, Inc.
311 Turner Street
Utica, New York 13501-5618

To the centennial of the
Adirondack Park

1892 - 1992

FOREWORD

I like Emerson's definition of a great story. He was at a literary luncheon in Boston hosted by Adirondack Murray's publisher. Murray asked him, "What makes a great story?" Emerson said, "A story which makes the average person both laugh and cry is a great story."

Some of the Adirondack stories I like to tell are printed here in the versions I use in performance. To me these stories open a whole world to the imagination. Here are the experiences, the dreams, the day-by-day lives of the Adirondacks' early settlers and visitors. These are the funny stories and tragic stories they told each other. Here we see the beginnings of Adirondack culture. Here, too, we catch glimpses of the Adirondacks our forefathers a century ago wanted to preserve for us when they created the Adirondack Park. I hope these stories will be read at many firesides and be good company.

—John Vinton
Brooklyn

ACKNOWLEDGMENTS

Many generous people have helped me with their advice, their suggestions for stories, their loans and gifts of books, their hospitality and friendship. I want to thank them.

Norman and Margery Aamodt, Lake Placid; Tom and Donna Amoroso, Childwold; Priscilla Angelo, Cranberry Lake; Jim and Ann Bailey, Plattsburgh; Alan Bartenhagen, Northern Roads Productions; Dick Beamish, Saranac Lake; Ted Blackman, Upper Saranac Lake; Ed Blankman, Adams; Parker and Judy Blatchford, Big Wolf Lake; Steve and Sylvia Boyce, Ticonderoga; Pat Brown, Watertown; Neal Burdick, Canton; Kent Busman, Camp Fowler; Bob and Helen Cackener, Gansevoort; Warder and Judy Cadbury, Indian Lake; Will and Elizabeth Clarkson and family, Windover Lake; Ben Coe, Tug Hill Commission; Sarah Comstock, Old Forge; Ted Comstock, Old Forge; Jim and Caroline Dawson, Peru; Jacques and Jeanne DeMattos, Saranac Lake; Maitland De Sormo, Saranac Lake; Bob and Ann Dreizler, Ilion; Harry and Betty Eldridge, South Meadow Farm Lodge; Bea Foley, Old Forge; Corey and Susan Folta, Lake Placid; Elizabeth Folwell and Tom Warrington, Blue Mountain Lake; Jan Frye and Jo Lathouse, Columbus; Bill and Therese Gibeau, Malone; Hamp Gillespie, Houston; Mack and Betsey Griswold, Fairport; Val Grosselfinger, Raquette Lake; Francis and Jean Hall, Inlet; George and Mary Heim, Garnet Hill Lodge; Leo Hollister, Houston; Freddy and Curly Hoyt, Baltimore; Gary and Bettye Hughes, Hannibal; Richard and Elaine Huyda, Ottawa; Paul Jamieson, Canton; Ray and Dickie Jenkins, Tupper Lake; Margaret Kastler, Lacona; Daisy Kelley, The Adirondack Museum; Howard Kirschenbaum, Raquette Lake; Richard Knight, Old Forge; Anne LaBastille, Wadhams; Jan and Helen LaRue, New Canaan; Diane Mantis, The Wawbeek; Larry and Lydia Miller, Belleville; Edith Mitchell, Tupper Lake; Irene Moehs, Old Forge; Brenda Parnes, Brooklyn; Joan Payne, Adirondack Discovery; Janice Peasley, Lake Pleasant; Jerold Pepper, The Adirondack Museum; Donna Pohl, Raquette Lake; Gordon L. Purdy II, Speculator; Stan Ransom, Clinton-Essex-Franklin Library System; Gary and Janet Reichert, Tupper Lake; Gayle Rettew, The Chapman Museum; Pete Sanders, Elk Lake Lodge; Frances Seaman, Long Lake; Michael Schames, New York; Gordon Sherman, Westport; Bob Simon, Cranberry Lake; Genevieve Sutter, Tupper Lake; Bill and Jane Thomas, Lowville; Breck and Julie Turner, Lake Placid; Paul and Sally Turo, Sandy Creek; William Vickers, Wanakena; Victor and Melissa Vito, Lake George; Carlin Walker, Westport; Clark Walz, Jefferson County Historical Society; Bob and Jackie Webb, Blue Mountain Lake; Don Williams, Gloversville; Isabella Worthen, Old Forge Library; Jeri Wright, Wilmington.

I also want to thank North Country Books for publishing this *Treasury*. Bob Igoe, president of the company, suggested several years ago that I put together a collection of stories. His daughter Sheila Orlin, who manages the firm, and Rob Igoe, Jr., general manager, made this book happen. Their art director John Mahaffy guided it through a demanding production process, and their typesetter Audrey Sherman took great care and truly mothered the book.

Finally, thank you George Davis and Larry and Lydia Miller. Larry, your woodburnings and drawings have given me not only pleasure but also new ways of seeing. I hope these pages bring you many new admirers.

TABLE OF CONTENTS

INTRODUCTION

The Centennial of the Adirondack Park—what a momentous occasion.

In an era when the earth's forest cover is being rapidly destroyed, and in a region of our nation where development pressures are intense, New Yorkers for a hundred years have been nurturing a wilderness, a sanctuary of nature, a place of adventure. No government has acted so boldly, dedicating one-fifth of its territory to the preservation of wildness. There is no finer example of New York's vision and greatness than our Adirondack Park.

Located in northern New York State, the Park's six million acres—as large as the entire state of Vermont—are a unique mix of public and private land. Geologically the Adirondacks are not part of the Appalachian Chain but rather a fist-like extension of an ancient and vast underground lava flow known as the Canadian Shield. Time and again the Adirondack extension has been thrust up and worn down and scoured by glaciers, leaving a landscape both awesome and sublime.

Historically the Park's people are most closely linked to northern New England where most of the earliest settlers came from. For people today the Park is not only a place of natural beauty but a symbol of hope—hope for a battered earth, hope that humans can live in harmony with their natural environment.

It was not always so. In the nineteenth century the Adirondacks were ravaged. Species after species of wildlife were exterminated for sport or profit. Millions of acres were stripped of their timber—the pine for ship masts, the hemlock for tannin, and the spruce for pulp, lumber and fine musical instruments. The slash dried to tinder and soon enormous fires blackened the skies for hundreds of miles. Photographs from the period show a devastated landscape unfit for recreation or habitation with soils eroding off mountainsides, once-bubbling streams dried up or clogged with slash and silt.

But even in this devastation lay promise. For today, after a century of public and private stewardship, the Adirondack Park has become a lush, world-renowned preserve of lakes and streams, forests and mountains. Once again it is home to bald eagles and peregrine falcons, yellow-cheeked voles, beaver, moose and lynx. Carefully managed forests and untrammeled wilderness co-exist with benefit for all. The Park is also home to nearly a quarter-million year-round and seasonal residents and is visited by millions of vacationers annually.

With enough money it might have been possible to purchase all the private lands within the Park and exclude residents. Or we might have gone to another extreme and exploited the full commercial potential of the Park with billboards and road-side honky-tonks. But these ultimate insults to the Creator did not occur. Instead we chose during the last hundred years to seek a balance between human domination and reverence for nature. It raises our hopes that the earth itself can one day be respected and cherished as a global park.

The eyes of the world are on us as the Adirondack Park enters its second century. Even as we celebrate this joyous centennial the political winds are blowing ill-will for the Park. Once again the citizens must lead; let us continue to be wise stewards.

In this *Treasury*, storyteller John Vinton ably captures the history and culture of the Adirondacks toward the close of the nineteenth century, at that critical time when we first began to realize what we were losing. These compelling and enduring stories remind us that the Adirondacks were, and remain, the domain of people as well as of wildness. And therein lies the secret the Adirondacks can tell the world.

—George D. Davis
Wadhams

BIRTH OF THE WATER LILY

Location: the Saranac lakes, Franklin County
Source: Charles M. Skinner, *Myths & Legends of Our Own Land* (1896)

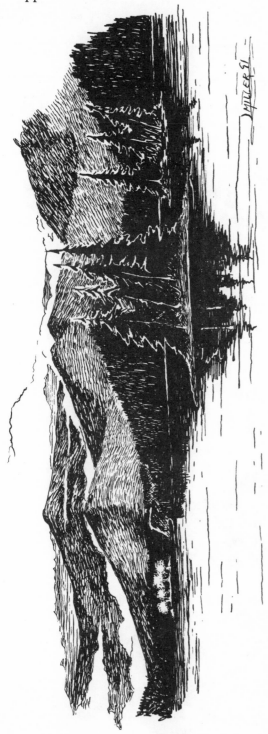

In the days before time the Saranac Indians hunted the lakes now named for them. The Lower Lake they called Lake of the Clustered Stars, and the Upper Lake they called Lake of the Silver Sky. Among their enemies were the Tahawi, who camped on the slopes of the Cloud Splitter, now called Mt. Marcy. Many are the tales of war between these tribes.

In the end the Tahawi were victorious, and the image of their chief, Adota, is graven in jagged rock on the cliffs above Lower Ausable Lake. The image of his grandson, The Star, rests beneath him. Both were etched in lightning by the thunder god. The Dark Cup, as this lake was called, was a place of solemn rites.

The Saranacs left a different mark, for their tales are as much of love as war. One year in the moon of green leaves their chief, Blazing Sun, came back the winner. He had many scalps. "The eagle screams!" he cried. "The Tahawi tremble and fly!" There was dancing and feasting.

When the feast was over and the boasting was going on, The Bird crept away. She loved Blazing Sun, but he had given his promise to another. Yet secretly, in his heart, he loved The Bird and not the one who held his pledge. The Bird knew this, but she was high-principled and of strong faith.

Blazing Sun saw her leave the circle. He followed her footprints. They led to the shore. Her canoe was just turning past the Isle of Elms. He pursued and found her on a high rock.

He left his canoe and tried to embrace her, but she drew back. He asked her to sing to him. She refused. It was not her place to sing to him. He ordered her. He

was Chief Blazing Sun. She looked at him. There was sadness in her face. Then she ran across the rock and hurled herself from the edge.

Blazing Sun sprang after her and swam with all his might. But she was gone. He called. There was no answer. He returned to camp and told his people what had happened. They searched but found nothing. While The Bird's family wailed, Blazing Sun moaned in his sleep.

On the morrow a hunter came running with strange news. Flowers were growing on the water! The people went in their canoes to see this new thing, flowers growing on water.

There in a cove by the Isle of Elms the water was covered with blossoms, some white, some yellow. The air was filled with their perfume. "But what is it?" they asked. "It was not so before."

That night Wise One lit the sacred pipe, and in the smoke that curled upward the Great Spirit spoke to him:

"It is your daughter, Oseetah. These are her spirit. The white is her purity, the yellow her love. Her heart will close when the sun departs and reopen when he returns. Remember, for it shall always be."

BILL GWINUP DOES IT

for Brenda Parnes

Location: St. Lawrence County, c. 1900

Source: Irving Bacheller, "A Tale of Two Burdens," *Century Magazine* (August 1908)

Bacheller (1859-1950) was a native of rural St. Lawrence County. He graduated from St. Lawrence University and settled in New York City, where he became a journalist and established America's first syndication service for newspapers. His stories of the North Country made him a best-selling author. The antagonism described here between rich landowners and native woodsmen was real at the turn of the century and led to many incidents, including murder.

You ask Milt Thomas. He'll tell ya. Cause half a day there I was a millynair. I was one a the biggest millynairs there is. But I give it up. All them folks shootin at ya?

Ya 'member John Calladay? Yeah, same one. Wal, he bought a lot a land up in Harewood. Didn't do nuthin but sit there all day'n'go fishin. Wouldn't even cut the wood off it. He had Courtney Laird cut the wood off his place an draw it over.

Wal, they was folks living there long fore Calladay. They veered how they had claims a one kind er nuther. They ben huntin them hills a hundred year, some of em.

But Calladay, he got right after em. Drove em out with a club. Like ya drive bulls out a barn yard. He went in there, knocked down their shanties.

An they kicked, I'll tell ya. Tried ta burn him out, one of em did. Took a shot at him. We heered plenty a talk.

But Calladay, he had his land covered. An Gabe Dorr made sure nobody got in. He's the one went crazy out'n the woods. Yeah. Got lost in the snow and went crazy.

Now fer two year Milt Thomas was in'n'out a court. An he lost everthin he had. One after nuther they turned him out. Hell, it wahnt but seventy acre he were claimin. An Calladay, he had half the county!

Wal, one day Gabe Dorr sends fer me. He says ta me, "Mr. Calladay wants ta see ya."

"Wants ta see me?" I says.

"Yeah," he says. "Wants ya ta work for him."

"Me work fer Calladay?"

Wal, he offers big money, an, wal,

times was bad. Worse'n we ever seen. So I calate I'll go over there, see what he wants.

So we go inside, me and Dorr. An right away I'm feelin under-civilized. Cause I got turned round gettin there an had ta come out through a cedar swamp. But Dorr says no, keep yer boots on. Mr. Calladay likes mud round the place. Makes it more camp-like.

He tells me ta set down. But these here chairs he's got in his room — An it's a big one. Ya could put, oh, I say . . . four a these rooms in there. Wal, the chairs is all covered in white. An they feel like they got two foot a moss in em. Not the kind a chair ya wanna get yerself in. Not round a man like Calladay. So I keep ta my feet and look at the buck heads.

I'm feeling like a man bout ta meet his first bear. I don know but what Calladay's got horns on him. Big diamons stead a eyes.

So I'm lookin round at the buck heads. An in he walks. Wal, ya could a tipped me over with a knittin needle. He's like . . . anybody. Bigger lookin I s'pose, with them boots. But he don look like no devil. No tail er nuthin.

"How are ya, Gwinup?" he says. He holds out his hand. Aint got no scaleys on it. "Glad ta have ya with us. Ben hearin a lot about ya."

Wal, that makes ya feel kind a swelled up. So we set down in them moss chairs. I'm thinkin I wouldn't mind it, havin one a his moss chairs. Right front a the stove's where I'd put it.

Calladay says, "I hear yer a good fisherman."

"I genrally have luck," I says.

"Let's try it," he says. "All I ask is ya do yer best." He lays his hand on me. "An I'll do what's right by you, Gwinup."

So I foller him down the hall, this long hall, down ta nuther room. He opens a door an pulls out a pair a top boots. "Here," he says, "try these." Good stout boots they is—and jes the fit.

He reaches in there again, pulls out a suit a clothes. Millynair clothes! He hands me a shirt softer'n the hind end of a coon. An pants. Good thick pants. An a big coat's got green squares wove on it. "I like my help ta dress good," he says.

Wal, they fit like a buck's britches. I'm gettin swelled up lookin at em. He comes back, gives me a lookover. "Very nice," he says. "Go wait'n the hall. I'll have em put up a luncheon." Cause that's what millynairs calls it when they et. They calls it "luncheon." I don know what's in it. But I was wonderin.

So Calladay comes back. An this time he's got a hat. A big hat. A pigskin hat. Big brim on it. An a white satin band. A cowboy hat! "Try that," he says. "Best hat there is fer the woods."

Wal, course I don say what I'm thinkin. Damndest hat ever was. But he's payin. Payin good. "You an me's bout of a size," I says.

"Yeah," he says. "We both dress bout a hundred eighty."

He goes out again. An this time he comes back wearin lumber boots, old lumber boots. He's got a shirt on no better'n the one I took off. An a hat worse'n Avah Bitters'. Trout flies hangin off it. Then his gal comes in with that "luncheon" done up in a paper. An I put it down the pack next his tackle and his raincoat. It was a big size. I could feel that.

Then—Ya won believe it. I jes stood there an looked. He takes holt the pack an swings it up on his back. I tell him that's my work. But he says no, he likes carryin a pack. He likes the exercise. An he pays good ta do what he likes. An if'n he gets tired, then he'll give it ta me.

"Okay," I says. I'm thinkin millynairs look okay, but they's bout as mooney as a cow in June. He gives me a couple cigar, too. Tells me smoke em anytime I like!

So I foller him downtrail. Aint got nuthin ta carry but a fishin pole. I'm walkin 'long, lookin round, watchin the trees blow. If my hound come along, he wouldn't a knowed me. I'm wonderin, mebby Calladay's gonna lay one a his millons on me. Wal, Lord knows he could do it, easy as I could toss a nickle.

Bym-by we come on a landin. But fore we git'n the boat, he gets out the tar oil, an he slicks his hands and his face. He slicks it on an slicks it on till he's the blackest, stickest man ever was. Course them city folk, they blow up like a dead cow if a fly bites em.

Wal, we fish downstream bout ten mile. Hardly say a word. He's fishin. I'm smokin.

Bym-by he says, "Pull up. We'll put across land ta camp." But he says leave the boat. Come back for it tomorra. He says take my time bout it, too. "Yes, sir!" I says. I'd about stood on my head if he asked.

He's bound ta carry that pack again. Dead game bout it. So I foller him downtrail, holdin the fishin pole an the trout. Swelled up I was like a millynair.

A half hour goes by an I hear somethin. I think mebby it's a deer. We stop an listen. He says, "You might sneak ahead, see what's there."

So I sneak ahead. This time he's hangin back about ten rod. I don hear nuthin. But I got the woods fear in my gizzard.

I hear water up ahead. I'm gettin thirsty, so I git down fer a drink—An that's when I see myself. Damn if I'm not the devil's image of Calladay!

He drops a tin cup beside me. "Here," he says. "Use that." I look up—an BANG! Off goes a rifle. I give a jump fer life an mother. An that water splashes up right where I'm gonna put my face.

I hear someone yellin. "Come near gettin it, didn't ya?" Wal, that's when I begin fillin up with useful knowledge. The swellin goes right out.

A man comes crackin down the hill. "Stand right where ya are!" he says. He's got a gun pointin. Calladay? He's settin on a log, face down, not sayin a word.

I'm thinkin supple now. An I come near dumpin them millons. Let him do his own cipherin.

"I'm Milt Thomas," the man says. "An I ben gunnin fer you fer two year."

"Wadda ya want?" I says.

"I want my land ya stole's what I want. Ya can give it back, er ya can be blowed off ta hell."

He pulls out a paper. He says it's a deed. He says fer me ta sign it an swear by it. An he's got me an Calladay covered so's he can get us in the shake of a buck's tail.

So I take the paper. It gives him seventy acre on the upper river. "It's the land ya stole!" he says. It's all done up 'ccordin ta law. Got a place ta sign. "My dad bought that land, an you busted the deed. Ya lawed me and my wife and kids ta the poor-house. We aint got nuthin left but a shanty."

So here's where I start talkin nice. "Ya got a pen?" I says.

"Right here." He pulls out a pen.

"I tell ya what, Thomas," I says, "I ben meanin ta do this, give yer land back. I don want no quarrel. It's jes—wal, it was a matter a principles."

So I write Calladay's name cross the bottom. An I make it good millynair writin— like a six-inch squirrel track.

"Tell yer guide ta witness it!" he says. So I hand it down ta Calladay, an he writes "Bill Gwinup" on it.

"No, Thomas, I don want no quarrel," I says. Then I do some more cipherin. "Tell ya what, Thomas," I says. "I'm real sorry bout yer wife'n'kids. You come back with me. Cause I'm gonna give you a check fer a thousand dollar. An that's fer the misses."

Wal, he comes right off'n his high horse. Puts on a big smile. Tells me he's glad ta hear it. How Gabe Dorr wouldn't let him git near. "Wal," I says, "I aint sayin but John Calladay's a low-down skunk." An I look down ta Calladay. "Aint that so?" An Calladay says, "Yes, sir." "But he's a man a his word. Aint that so?" An Calladay says, "Yes, sir." "An when I say ya can have yer land back an a check fer a thousand dollar, I mean it."

"An no bad feelins?" he says.

"No bad feelins. You take yer land an you take the check, an if you have any more bother out a me, you come back with yer gun."

So we shake hands, an he starts up the hill ta git his pack. An I do some more cipherin.

"Hold on, Thomas!" I says. "My man here'll carry that pack for ya. He's dead game fer carryin a pack. He was sayin so today. We'll leave mine here. He can come back for it tomorra. Take his time bout it, too. May as well leave the fishin pole an the trout."

So I send Calladay up the hill. He comes back draggin a sack full up bout fifty pound a gear. "This is rather heavy," he says.

"Wal, that's what I pay ya for, Gwinup!"

So he moans'n'groans an gits it up on his back. An all the way uptrail he's huffin' n'puffin. "Get movin!" I says. I treat him like a cow dog. "Mr. Thomas here's waitin fer his money."

He's got close on fifty pound in that sack. I calate that's about one pound fer ever one a his millons. I tell Thomas I'm gonna fire him. "Aint no better'n'a weasel. An not half as smart!" An I say it good'n'loud. "Aint that so?"

Wal, bym-by we come where the river's crossin the trail. There's a boat t'other side. So I tell Calladay go out'n'fetch it. "The water's rather deep," he says.

"Wadda ya think I pay ya for, Gwinup?"

So he goes out there. Up ta his neck. His eyes buggin out. Arms battin the water. Snortin like a pig. "Go on! Go on!" I says. Next thing he gets his foot stuck in a clay hole. An when he gets back, his boots're closhin.

So me an Thomas, we ride over. Calladay does the rowin. An all the way back he's closhin in them lumber boots. An I know fer a fact he wants ta quit. But he's too damn scairt.

So we git back ta camp, an me an Calladay, we go inside. He's drippin'n'squashin. His gal comes out an screams at him. All that fly dope, he looks like a bull moose.

Wal, he takes me up ta his room. He's got a big desk up there. Lot a drawers in it. An a big lamp with a fancy glass. "Yer a damn tyrant!" he says.

He pulls out his checkbook. A big one. "Ya shouldn't a lost yer temper," he says. He writes the check. An I give it a good lookover, make sure it's got the oughts where they go. "You most broke my back!" he says.

"An you, ya devil!" My blood's gittin up. "You most broke my head. You give me yer load, I give ya mine. An here on I'm wearin my own hat'n'coat. Cause these a yers is more'n likely ta git full up a holes."

An that's how I got Milt Thomas his land back.

CROSSING THE CARRY

Location: the swamp between Rock Pond and Salmon Lake, Hamilton County, 1860s

Source: William H. H. ("Adirondack") Murray, *Adventures in the Wilderness; or, Camp-Life in the Adirondacks* (1869)

Visitors to the Adirondacks have left many "crossing the carry" stories. This is the most vivid. Murray (1840-1904) was pastor of the Congregational church in Meriden, Connecticut, when he wrote the story. In 1869, when it was published in book form, he was pastor of the prestigious Park Street Church on Beacon Hill in Boston. There he became the second most renowned preacher in America after Henry Ward Beecher of Brooklyn. His Adirondack stories were an instant best-seller. His guide, John Plumley, was a native of Long Lake.

Also from Murray: "Farewell to John Plumley," 149; "Phantom Falls," 141

Further reading: Warder H. Cadbury, "Introduction," *Adventures in the Wilderness*, reprint ed. (1970), 11-75; Harry V. Radford, *Adirondack Murray* (1906)

First I want to emphasize that John and I are not newcomers to the wilderness. John was born here, and he and I have boated for hundreds of miles through this meshwork of waterways. Thus, when I describe our adventure of crossing the carry, I want you to remember that this was the exception and not the rule of our journeys.

It began about midday on Rock Pond. It was August. Suddenly a storm blew up.

Froth and splashing rain began to hit the boat. We shot through lily pads, pulled the boat ashore, turned it bottom-up, and crawled under as a flood of gray water swept over us.

For a time we lay there, safely sheltered, as the rain drummed over our heads. But while we were talking, a tickling sensation on my right side told me water was gathering beneath us. Reluctantly we crawled back out into the downpour.

John patted the boat. "She's got a good roof, Mr. Murray. No doubt about that. But I reckon her cellar needs some repair."

Ahead of us for some two miles lay an uncut carry, the first half of which ran through a swamp. "John," I said as we stood looking at each other across the boat, "this rain is wet!"

"Generally is, Mr. Murray." He was already getting our things together. "Better load light. I'll come back fer what's left."

"No, John. This baggage is going over in one load, sink or swim." I dragged the pork bag out from under the boat. "One load, John, survive or perish!"

I slung the packbasket over my back. It was thirty inches by forty and loosely filled with plates, coffee, salt—the usual items of camp cooking. Only it felt like eighty-pounds weight. On top of it John lashed a knapsack full of bullets, powder, and clothing.

My rubber blanket he let hang round my neck. On one shoulder he balanced the oars and paddles—with a frying pan and gridiron dangling from the blades. On my other shoulder he balanced the rifle. And on the end of that he hung a pair of boots, a coffee pot, and a sack of flour. He put the pork bag in one hand and the bucket of leftover trout on two free fingers.

If you can imagine a man so loaded, forcing his way through a cedar swamp, jiggling and jangling like a broken clock, sinking to his knees in moss or picking his way on roots covered with mud and slippery beyond belief—well, if you can picture that, you have me daguerreotyped in your mind.

Yet for some dozen rods I got on famously. I was just congratulating myself when a root gave way under me and I plunged headlong into the mud. The gridiron banged me in the head. I muttered something—not exactly religious—and fished the frying pan out of the slime. This time I lashed the gridiron to my belt.

Before another fifty rods had passed under me, the packbasket weighed a hundred and twenty pounds at least. And where was the center of gravity? In front? In back? To the side? I found where it wasn't—several times.

The pork bag dragged on my arm as if there were whole country hams in it. And the oars spread out in the exact form of an X no matter what I did. If I went one side of a tree, they went the other. If I backed up, they got tangled in the brush. And if I stumbled, the confounded things came down on my neck and pinned me in the slime.

The roots I was hopping on grew farther apart, the mud deeper, the blazed trees less frequent. The rain simply would not let up. Hymns began running through my mind. I remember one in particular: "O, had I the wings of a dove!"

At length I reached an impossible pass—an oozy slough crossed only here and there by slippery roots. I climbed a stump, surveyed the morass, and gave a leap. The packbasket pressed me forward. By now it weighed well over two hundred pounds. I caught myself for a second, till the oars swung back and hurled the boots in my face. Then my moccasins began to slide out from under me. So I skipped to another root—the coffee pot struck me in the ribs—and another. Suddenly the trout

leaped out of the pail. The gridiron got uneasy and banged my legs like a steam flapper.

Now I want you to understand I am conscienciously opposed to dancing. What would my deacons say? I never danced as a young man. What would my wife say? Yet here I was out in the middle of the woods doing a hornpipe in the rain.

The trout were leaping about my head as if to prove they were in their native element. The gridiron was in such rapid motion I couldn't distinguish the bars. The pork bag felt like it had a litter of nervous pigs in it. Indeed, everything I carried seemed endowed with its own powers of locomotion.

Finally I looked about for a soft spot to rest myself. I fully intended to do the thing gracefully. But out my feet flew from under me, and—well, I don't recall I ever sat down quicker. The motion was very decided.

Once again the oars were astride my neck. The trout pail was bottom-up, its contents strewn about. One piece of pork lay at my side. Another was stuck in the mud some ten feet off. It looked rather out of place. Somehow my boots had got to hanging from a limb overhead. Well, it was a dry limb. And the rifle stood muzzle-down in the mud. Now that struck me as a good idea—no danger of its falling over and breaking the stock.

I have long believed that every gentleman should have something solid beneath him. And since my present seat appeared to have no bottom whatever, I slid the gridiron beneath me. I was just thinking how many uses a gridiron can be put to when I heard John forcing his way through the brush. It would never do to let him see me like this. With a mighty effort I managed to reach a spruce limb and pull myself free of the suction.

"John! John, over here!" I disengaged myself from the pack. "Put the boat down." I yanked the rifle out of the mud. "I've found a splendid place here. And I think the rain is letting up."

He leaned the boat against a tree and emerged from under his burden. "How ya gettin on, Mr. Murray?"

"Capitally, John. Capitally!" By now I was leaning against a tree. "The carry is actually quite level—when you get down to it. But I was feeling a little out of breath and thought I'd rest a while."

Something caught his eye overhead. "Mr. Murray, what's yer boots doin up there?"

"Doing? Why, you wouldn't expect me to drop them in all this mud, would you?"

"No, I don't suppose you'd . . . But, but what's this?" He reached down and pulled a trout out of the ooze.

"Oh, that. I thought I heard something drop."

He looked ahead of him. "What in thunder is that? Is that pork, Mr. Murray?"

"John, haven't you noticed? This carry seems to be littered with pork. I wouldn't be surprised to find a piece anywhere." To prove my point I dug a moccasin in the mud and kicked a two-pound bit his way. "See? It's lying all over the place, loose."

John had a good laugh over that, but my turn came. He turned halfway round and I saw his jacket was caked with mud clear up to his hat. "John! Do you always lie on your back when you cross a carry?"

"Ya know, Mr. Murray, I always tell my wife ta make my clothes a ground color. But this time I think she laid it on a bit thick!"

We fished out a tin plate, and I scraped him down. "John, if you'll spear my boots off that limb, I'll go get the pork." He took one of the oars as I plunged into the ooze.

I had just about succeeded in concentrating the meat all in one place when I heard a groan. My boots were still in the tree. And not only that. The oars and two paddles had joined them in the branches. John was red in the face and whirling the frying pan round his head.

"Go to it, John! When you've got the rest of the baggage up there, I'll pass up the boat and we'll make camp!"

The words were barely off my lips when John lost his footing, and the frying pan careened through the branches like a bird with a broken wing. Now his blood was really up, and the bombardment began in earnest. He laid hold of the coffee pot. I followed with the gridiron and the flour. Then the fishing basket and the bag of bullets. The air was full of missiles—plates, oar locks, the axe, pieces of pork. Every-thing was flying at once. Then John hurled the iron kettle, which struck the tree like a forty-pound shot, and the whole baggage came tumbling down on our heads.

We picked up our articles, tied them on again, and pressed forward. In an hour's time, just as the rain finally did cease, we reached the margin of the swamp and cut our way through the last opposing thicket.

Salmon Lake! The dreaded carry was crossed.

THE HUCKLEBERRY PICKERS

Location: The St. Regis River, Franklin County, c. 1880

Source: Philander Deming, *Tompkins and other Folks* (1885)

Deming (1829-1915) grew up in Burke, Franklin County, and remained in the area for most of his twenties. He put himself through the University of Vermont, then settled in Albany where he became America's first court stenographer and, later, a nationally acclaimed writer.

Also from Deming: "The Captin's Tale," 91; "Little Willie," 45

Further reading: Philander Deming, "A Shorthand Pioneer," *The Stenographer* (March 1910), 101-02; — —, *The Story of a Pathfinder* (1907); — —, "Growing Old," *Scribner's Magazine* (March 1915), 372-74: Ken Lawless, "Lost: A Major Writer," *Adirondack Life* (Sept.-Oct. 1981), 23-25: Thomas P. O'Donnell, "The Secret Passion of Philander Deming," *NAHO* (winter 1979), 13-15; Abe C. Ravitz, "Philander Deming: Howells's Adirondack Prodigy," *New York History* (Oct. 1955), 404-12

Along the St. Regis River there's a mountain called Blue. It was lumbered years ago, and by the 1870s huge tracts of huckleberries grew there. Farmers used to come with their families and pick the berries. They'd camp for a few days and visit and make quite a holiday of it.

But one summer a boy was lost, Andrew Garfield. He was fourteen. He went out on a Thursday afternoon to hunt partridges. When he didn't return, quite a disturbance was made. A dozen men went looking for him, but it was already dark and they couldn't find his tracks. "Ya might just as well ben walkin through a mountain a molasses," one of them said, "as walk through them woods at night."

The next morning several parties went out, firing guns. They thought they heard a shot upriver. They fired again and again but heard nothing more.

The news spread rapidly, and a good many people arrived. Two surveyors were sent for. They said the boy was probably following the river. That gunshot must have been his. So they set out with a party of four.

It happens I was visiting the family homestead at the time. My brother Edward lives there now. It's about twenty miles from the mountain. Andrew went out for partridges on Thursday. We heard about it Friday afternoon. And early Saturday morning Edward hitched his team to a lumber wagon and we set out.

Such a beautiful morning it was, soft and fragrant. After a time we met a man walking our way—Sam Curley. He climbed in the wagon and told us there was a new joke down where he lives.

"Tom Powell sold his old cow. He got Bill Worden ta buy it. Tom Powell had that cow a good ten year, but he said she was six year old.

"Wal, the cow aint got but one horn. An that oughta tole Bill right there. She was so old her horn jus fell off.

"Wal, Bill gets her home an looks her over. An that's when he seed the wrinkles. You know a wrinkle comes out on a cow's horn one a year. Wal, they was thirteen

wrinkles on the horn. So Bill goes back ta Tom Powell an tells him he's a liar. The cow was thirteen. She wahnt six.

"An Tom said ta him, 'Bill Worden, you are a numbskull.' An that's the Lord's truth. He said, 'Bill Worden, you are a numbskull. Look at that cow. She aint got but one horn. She's makin wrinkles fer two. So all of em, they're comin out on the one horn.' An Bill Worden believed it!"

We reached the huckleberry plains about eleven o'clock. It was already crowded —twenty or thirty teams, nearly a hundred people.

We pitched our tent and tied the horses to the back of Ed's wagon. No word yet from the surveyors. They'd been out nearly twenty-four hours. A peddler rode up and we told him how things stood.

At night fires were built in front of the tents, and the men gathered round to sing and tell stories. Some talked about the war—camping on the Potomac.

It must have been an hour after dark when we heard shots in the woods about a quarter mile away. Immediately the men fired guns in camp.

There was a scream as Andrew's mother ran out of her tent. She was a small woman with light hair. She wore a blue calico dress. The women tried to comfort her. Then her husband came up. "Don't cry, Jane. Mebby he aint dead, after all."

A few minutes later two men came out of the woods. They were part of the surveyor's party. They said they found Andrew's tracks. He was heading south in a line with the river about two miles this side of it. They found where he'd picked berries. They said he'd probably get to the river, and if he did, he'd keep by the side of it. Someone should take a boat up there and call for him.

But the men wondered if he could still be alive. It was three nights now. A red-haired man spoke up. He was the one who said it was "like walkin through molasses walkin them woods at night." He said it was possible. He thought Andrew was still alive. "I won't be sleepin a wink. I'll be thinkin bout that boy the whole time." The company began drifting away, and by midnight all that could be thought of was said.

The next day was Sunday, so most of the crowd stayed in camp. There were nearly three dozen tents by now. Someone suggested a church service, but no one wanted to lead it. So a few singers—and we had good ones about!—they got folks together from time to time to sing hymns.

About five o'clock I heard voices off towards the river. People were running that way. There was shouting and clapping. In the middle of the crowd was the red-haired man, and standing beside him was a light-haired boy.

Andrew's mother shot from her tent like a cannon ball. She fell down. Someone helped her up. When she got to Andrew she threw her arms around his neck and pulled him down on the ground and wept. Andrew cried, too, but he was clearly unhappy about the scene.

The red-haired man had taken his boat at dawn and gone upriver. It was mostly stillwater. He went a dozen miles, calling and listening. About noon he turned around and started down again.

A little before five he was nearing the camp. Now and then the wind brought him the sound of women singing. He came round the last bend, feeling dejected. But then the grass stirred. A head popped up. It was Andrew!

"I tell ya, boys, when that grass wiggled an his head popped up an I seed it was Andrew. Settin there like little Moses in the bulrushes! I tell ya, boys, it made my hair pull. An he wahnt scairt. He jest wanted a ride home."

Was he hurt? No.

He must be starved. Oh, he wahnt hungry much. But after supper he admitted he was "a little bit holler" toward the end. Still, berries and wintergreen and birch bark do all right for a few days.

But how could he sleep? "It slept itself," he said. The trouble was keepin awake. He liked it. He liked it first rate.

He heard the guns, but they got his head turned. He heard them in one direction, then another. He fired his own gun, but he lost the caps and couldn't fire any more. The next day he struck the river and when he saw how it was, he came back.

There was a farmer in the crowd named Pinkham. When he heard Andrew was missing, he made up slips of paper and fastened them to the trees as he picked: TOBIAS PINKHAM LOST. If he turned up missing, some hunters were to follow the signs, and if they found him alive, he'd pay a reward. They had their choice, too. He'd pay them in money or maple sugar.

NANCE'S BABY

Location: Warren County, c. 1880

Source: Jeanne Robert Foster, *Neighbors of Yesterday* (1916)

Foster (1879-1970) grew up in Minerva and Chestertown. During her teens she helped her father draw logs for lumbercamps. At the age of 17 she married a family friend, an insurance executive, and during her twenties, thirties, and forties she moved in the art and literary worlds of London, Paris, Boston, and New York.

Also from Foster: "The Last Tarrin'n'Featherin," 85; "The Lumberjack's Tale," 49; "The Old Church," 133; "Sonny's Coat," 71

Further reading: Noel Riedinger-Johnson, "Jeanne Robert Foster, 1879-1970," in Foster, *Adirondack Portraits* (1986), xxi-xli

Son: I knew them lumber shanties. My mom cooked for twenty men in one of em.

Months'd go by she wouldn't see another woman. She'd get pale an forget things an have strange fancies. She'd jump when icicles fell off the roof. An if a panther screamed, she'd run'n'bar the door.

Mother: Oh, now! I had you. You boys kept me comp'ny. I never went clean crazy like Nance Hills.

Son: Nance Hills?

Mother: You 'member. She kept the Byrd Pond shanty. She used ta come over'n'play with you.

Son: It was six miles across a cedar swamp. But she came over — what time she had, anyway — she came over on foot and sat with mother.

Mother: She liked to play with the boys. She used ta build things with em. One time she told me,

Nance: I ache so.
                I aint the same since little Jimmie died. I ache so.
                I steeped herbs. But the pain don't go.
                I told Miss Tripp when I went home last year. She said she was the same way, years back, when she lost one.
                It's baby fever, she said. It comes when ya lose em. Or they jes grow up'n'go away. Sometimes it comes when yer sick and lonely. The spell comes on. An ya sit an ache an ache. An don't know rightly where.
                An ya have dreams a babies. Daytime even. Ya see em. They come play on the floor.
                An food don't taste. An ya can't cry even.
                Ya feel a little head on yer arm, and hans . . .

Mother: She sat a time.

Nance: I've hoped'n'hoped fer anuther.

Mother: I got up an stirred the fire and made her drink a cup a tea.
                Then, one day I heard the men talking: "There's a baby at The Forks!"
                Nance has a baby?
                They said they looked in. A cradle was rocking on the floor.
                Poor thing, I thought, She must've had a hard time without a woman ta help her.
                So the first good day I rode over. Nance met me at the shanty door. Her face was sunshine.

Nance: Sh-h-h. He's gone ta sleep.

| Mother: | We sat by the stove an talked an talked. An all the while she stitched and laughed and showed me fixins mothers make fer babies. |
| | I asked ta see him. |

| Nance: | If ya don't mind, I'll let him be. He was sick last night. |

Mother:	I thought it queer I couldn't see him. But something kept me still.
	I rode home through the swamp. She stood there, watching me. Her red hair was wrapped in a bright blue shawl. It put me in mind of a picture at the Catholic church.
	The snows were deep that year. I couldn't get back till spring.
	The strange thing was, no one ever saw the baby. An they couldn't get a word outta Nance's man. He cursed when they asked him.
	One man said he watched by the window. An when Nance was

alone, she took the baby out an cuddled it an nursed it.

But no one ever heard the baby cry.

One day in spring her man rode in fast.

Nance's man: Can you come over? Nance is awful sick.

Mother: I got up behind. But we had ta walk the horse most a the way in the ankle slush. When we got there, Nance was wild with fever.

I made her easy. Then I went ta tend the baby—

I saw the crib there—

I turned the quilt—

It wasn't a baby. It was a doll. Made of rags an cloth. She dressed it an nursed it. A baby made of rags an cloth.

I picked it up. I couldn't help myself. I swear it felt warm.

Then it moved. I screamed an dropped it. I swear it moved—just like a baby moves.

Her man came up ta me.

Nance's man: I couldn't stop her.

Mother: Nance screamed. I went'n'put the kettle on.
                        When it was over, she slept.
                        I washed her baby. And dried him off. And wrapped him. And
                     laid him on her arm.

Nance's man: Is she all right?

Mother: Sh-h-h. Don't wake her.

Nance's man: He looks like someone. I think my mom.

Mother: We heard chains outside. The men were back. The horses ran to
                     the barn. The kitchen door banged open.

Lumberjack: Hey! Where's the grub?

Mother: Sh-h-h. It's a boy.

MR. ROOSEVELT

Location: Route 28N (approximately), Essex and Warren Counties, September 13-14, 1901

Source: Eloise Cronin Murphy, *Theodore Roosevelt's Night Ride to the Presidency* (1977). Copyright © 1977 by the Adirondack Museum of the Adirondack Historical Association. Retold by permission.

Vice-President Theodore Roosevelt was hiking on Mt. Marcy when a runner arrived to tell him President McKinley was dying. His rush to the train station at North Creek made headlines across the country and became an Adirondack legend. The ride was accomplished in three relays, the last driven by Mike Cronin over sixteen miles of wet winding road.

We were expecting him a lot sooner. A lot sooner. I got word about noon ta have everything ready for quick work. An that's what I did. I hitched up my span a blacks, Frank'n'Dick. They're fast steppers, an they know that road well as I do. They make the trip six times a week summer.

Like I say, we got the call about noon. An we waited. All afternoon we waited. We ate supper. An then I got fooled several times. There was a dance up at the Kay's, and after midnight people began driving home. I thought each of em was Mr. Roosevelt. The night was perfectly black. There was a misty rain coming down.

We thought sure Orrin'd get him here by two. But two o'clock came'n'went. Mr. Loeb had a special train waiting for him at North Crick. He called'n'called. The

whole country was waiting. Then—I remember it was 2:15—he called ta say McKinley was dead.

First thing, I told everyone not ta say a word. No sense gettin him more anxious.

Course, by now everyone was straining ta catch the first sight. An finally at three
o'clock Orrin Kellogg pulled him up. Why he didn't hustle him quicker I'll never
know. Nothing was said, just the necessary words, no demonstration. Folks just
stood'n'watched.

He climbed up beside me. Someone asked where ta put the lantern. I said it'd be
a bother on the dashboard, so Mr. Roosevelt spoke right up. "Here," he said, "give
it to me." An that settled the matter.

He's got ta be one a the nerviest men I ever saw. We were coming down a hill. It's a slippery hill, an it was the blackest night I ever saw. I couldn't even see the horses, only a few spots where the light fell. One a the horses stumbled. It's a ticklish bit a road. I said we better hold back. "No, no," he said. "That doesn't matter! Push ahead!"

An another time. We were coming round a sharp curve dug out a the hill. Now we could a ben pitched seventy-five or a hundred feet. I said we better slow down. "Not at all," he said. "I'm not afraid if you aren't. Push on!" Well, all I can say is, we were lucky. We didn't meet another team, not a single one.

He didn't say much. He looked sad to me. Mostly he was thinking. All he said was, "Keep up the pace!" He held his watch out front a that lantern an asked how much farther it was. I don't think I'll ever drive that road again without hearing his voice. "Push along, Mike! Hurry up, Mike! Faster, Mike!"

An then, after all that hurry'n'bother, when we got ta the Bibbey farm, he said ta stop. It's a flat stretch about two miles outside North Crick.

Oh, I forgot something. We had a Dr. Moore from White Plains. He was stayin at Nathan's camp on Balfour Lake. He came up ta me and he said he'd pay me fifty dollars ta let him drive the President ta North Crick. Imagine! Me let a novice drive

the President of the United States ta North Crick on a night like that!

Well, he got down an took a few steps an relieved himself. Then he straightened his tie and smoothed out his suit. "Might be some notables," he said.

We came over that bridge like thunder. We flew down Main Street. He jumped out before I stopped. Mr. Loeb handed him the telegram. An that's when he knew he was President.

We made the trip in an hour an forty-one minutes. Now that beats the next best time by a good quarter hour. I know cause it's a record I set myself with another two-seater, only in daylight. An it would a been five minutes quicker if he didn't need ta spruce up.

LITTLE WILLIE

Location: the northern foothills, 1850s?
Source: Philander Deming, *Adirondack Stories* (1880)
Also from Deming: "The Captain's Tale," 91; "The Huckleberry Pickers," 31

All night long lanterns and torches had flashed about the house and barn and behind logs and brush. The patches of snow that lingered in spite of the rain gave evidence that every foot of the clearing had been trampled over. Men were still poking at logs and bog holes.

"It stands ta reason a little chap like that couldn't get out a this clearin. I say he's half a mile a the house. Ya give me six men, I'll find him."

But what if Willie had crossed the brook? Then the whole wilderness lay before him.

A rough wagon came up the road and through the gate. It stopped in front of the house. There was a hush as the driver helped a large, coarse-featured woman climb down. He held her arm as she climbed the stoop and went in the house. The men crowded round the door and windows. Some had a reverent look on their faces. Others were snickering.

After a brief seance with a teacup she went outdoors and walked along the hollow. Here and there she dipped her cup in a puddle of melting snow. The neighbors watched her every move.

"The dear darlin's somewhere . . . there." She swung her arm in a vague half circle. Then she turned. "There's a black baste a-standin o're that swait child! Why weren't they looking? Why were they standing around like this?

Dan caught that. This was no way to find the boy. Following an old woman around the yard? Jim said he'd sell out and leave if they disgraced the town and chased after that she-devil any longer.

But an older man spoke up. "Inasmuch as some thinks as how she can tell, and some thinks as how she can't, so it were thought better fer ta go an fetch her. An let everybody satisfactory emselves. An no fault found. An everythin done fer the boy."

The fortune woman went back to the house, held a final seance with her teacup and declared the boy was half a mile away. But they better look quick, "before the black baste takes that poor neglected darlin." After this she was helped back in the wagon, and Jake drove her home.

At last the word was given, and a line more than half a mile long swung out from the road, diagonally across the stubble field, and toward the woods. Each man marched twenty feet from his neighbor, eyeing all the ground between. Then the platoon swept through the trees bordering the clearing. They doubled back, making semicircular swaths deeper and deeper into the forest. Partridges started up and whirred away.

In one direction the limit of the march was a river too broad for a four-year-old to cross. In the other, the limit was set by the colonel. By late afternoon the woods had been thoroughly searched for two miles. The colonel said it was all he could think of to do. The men returned, tired and hungry.

Then rumors began. Suspicious glances were turned on Willie's father. He was a bobcat when he got mad. Maybe he killed the boy. "Things is tremendous queer," they said.

When Dan heard the rumors, he denounced the wretch who started them. Who was it? The fortune woman? Superstitious fools were always suspicious. But Dan could not stay the rising tide. "Them's as lost can find." The men began searching the barn to see if a body was buried there.

Willie's father was no coward. As soon as the rumors reached him he called a meeting at the schoolhouse down the road. A hundred men crowded in—woodsmen, farmers, hunters. They sat and lolled on the benches. More than half thought John had killed the boy, and they watched closely as he approached the teacher's desk and turned to face them.

He said he had no knowledge who started the rumors, and he didn't want to know. But he asked his accusers to think, where was the evidence? There wasn't any. It was . . . There was a twitching of his face, which he instantly controlled.

Someone was saying he killed the boy. How could he do that? Kill his own son? He appealed to his friends. His face twitched again.

The men sprang from the benches. A few put their hands on John's shoulders. They said they'd known John for twenty years. He was as honest a man as could be found. And he was hard hit by the loss of his boy.

By now there was no prospect of finding Willie alive, so the search was given up. The men decided to wait three days till the snow was gone, then look for the body.

When John got home, he wept. The search was given up. Willie, little Willie was gone. Little Willie, whom he loved the best of anything on earth . . .

John was an upright man. The accusations against him stung his heart. He was a church member without reproach. But it became evident his speech had done no good. As the three days went by, the heads of Whiskey Hollow discussed the probability of his guilt. There would be a thorough overhauling of that house and barn!

There might have been an arrest if sentiment could have served as proof. Deacon Beezman, who lived out on the main road, said he "wasn't gonna waste any more a his time lookin fer the boy. The last time, John sat home readin a newspaper. If that wasn't actin guilty, what was?"

Excitement ran high as the morning of the third day approached. Men arrived from great distances to join the final search. Eight miles up the river Logan Bill left his cabin and took to the woods toward the gathering spot. It was cold and damp. He kept by the stream so as to avoid the brush, and he looked for signs of the panther he'd heard screaming that night.

About nine o'clock, when he was three miles from John's clearing, he saw a bundle of clothing. He went over and nudged it with his foot. A face appeared. It was Willie.

The boy was curled up, pale and lifeless, as cold to the touch as the ground he lay on. Logan choked as he lifted the body. It felt so light. He'd never held a child before.

It took two hours to carry Willie home.

Logan noted where the boy had climbed and struggled. Through fog and snow, for three miles he'd come, crying, calling for his father, so utterly alone under those vast, dark trees. Cold, hungry, calling. "Daddy, where are you? Daddy, where are you? Where are you?" Feeling his way over roots and stones till finally he was too tired to go on, and lying down for a while, he died.

Speaking no word, Logan Bill crossed the clearing. Groups of men were searching about the barn. Instantly they stopped. They came forward. Silently they gathered round and looked at the little white face. "Where'd ya find him?" they asked. A blanket was spread, and Logan laid his burden down.

Now John came out. There was a deeper hush as the crowd parted for him. The men looked to see how he'd take it. He stood there lion-like. Then he looked around, and to some his eye struck like a dagger.

A half hour passed. The crowd went away in twos and threes, asking themselves how such a tiny fella could get that far from home.

Services were held the next day. The whole neighborhood was there. At last John wept openly. And in the afternoon little Willie was laid to rest.

THE LUMBERJACK'S TALE

for Warder Cadbury

Location: told at Thirteenth Lake, Warren County, 1890s

Source: Jeanne Robert Foster, *Neighbors of Yesterday* (1916)

This is a story Foster heard at the lumbercamp on Thirteenth Lake, where she was helping her father draw logs. The Indian, Sabael, was born in Maine in 1747. He died in 1855 while on his way through the woods from Thirteenth to Indian Lake. His body was found in Indian Lake, and his dog's body in the woods nearby. Foul play was suspected, but no evidence was ever found. In early spring a sharp wind often drives down the narrow valley of Thirteenth Lake, causing sounds that resemble shrieks and moans.

Also from Foster: "The Last Tarrin'n'Featherin," 85; "Nance's Baby," 35; "The Old Church," 133; "Sonny's Coat," 71

Further reading: Robert Norton, "Sabael Benedict, Indian Pioneer," *Adirondac* (Dec. 1989), 16-18, 24

Oh, an how he loved that axe. Loved that axe! Always filin it an rubbin it. He rubbed oil on there with his bare hands. An then he took it ta bed with him! You ever tried sleepin with a axe in yer bed?

Course others of em did it. Not jus them Canucks.

Wal, that's what we guessed he was—Canuck. He talked Frenchy. But we didn't know enough bout him ta hold in one hand.

Cept the boss favored him. An he was good. Ya knew it when he stepped up to a tree an planted his feet, ya knew he was good. Yeah. Ya had ta keep two horses on him drawin logs.

An when the sun caught that axe blade—Wal, course you know weeks go by here,

weeks an no sun—But when the sun come out, it caught that axe an turned it blue. A cold kind a blue. An the chips flyin off, they looked like sparks.

Yeah, he was good. Cordy! Arms hard as the hammers a hell!

He set on that bunk there, rubbin, rubbin. All hell breakin loose. Most Canucks, they brag. They brag bout how big the log jams is up north. Not Savree. He jest set there rubbin, rubbin.

I asked him once where he ben workin. On the Saranacy? North River? He said somethin Frenchy an walked off.

Wal, after the sheriff took him, that's when we got ta puttin two an four up together.

First off, one night—must a ben end October, first a November—we was talkin bout old Sabael. Cause he was old and had all that gold.

He had a shack down by the sandbar. Wahnt nuthin but a pile a logs stood on end like a tee-pee. Ya see smoke comin out, an when ya didn't, ya knew he was on his traplines. But he didn't go out much.

He was the last a his tribe herebouts. A fightin Iroqouis. Ha! Talk bout the hammers a hell! He had a nose got broke, an it looked like the devil's anvil.

Ya'd go down there an ya'd see fox skins hangin out, rows on em. An mink an otter. Wolves. Bear. An painters! He had a painter one time more'n'nine foot from the end a the nose ta his tail, end a his tail. Nine foot! That's from where yer settin clear out the door. Varmints like that runnin round the woods all night! Makes ya think twice bout goin ta the outhouse.

The company let him stay cause when the company come in, he set some fires. Least that's what they said. An then he put em out real good. So the company

figgered they better let him stay, keep the fires out. An once a week the cook took him Christian grub in a pail. They said he was a hundred'n'twenty. Wal, he looked it.

Now thing was he wouldn't trade cept fer gold. He wouldn't trade fer no money, no credit. Jest gold. An he never spent a piece of it. He go ta town, trade his fur, pick up corn meal, tea, an molasses. An he go back in the woods. So all of us—ever jack from Thirteenth ta Newcomb—we all knowed there was a sack a gold round here somewheres, hid. An that's a sack a gold got talked about on a cold night.

Now what we remember was how Savree—Wal, he didn't look up precisely. But he stopped rubbin that blame axe. Now it aint somethin ya see always, but ya can tell when a man's listenin.

Then the first big snow come after that. Ha! Ya'd set yer pants on a hook at night, an they be still swingin when the boss banged the stove. An ever two week we head out fer the Crick. The boss give us half a day ever two week.

Cept Savree. He'd wait till we was outta here, an he'd go hide his pay. Never spent it, jest hid it. I say he hid it in a tree, seein how the ground was froze. Others of em, they said a cave.

He never took a drink. Never chewed tobaccy. He got thirteen dollar ever two week like us. Oh, mebby he got a dollar more. An he waited till we was out a here, an he hid it. Jest like Sabael.

One time the preacher come—Father Grimley. Come ta say prayers. Savree reached down his pants pocket an pulled out a coin. One coin!

Wal, wahnt long after, we get back from the Crick and Savree's out on the lake. The cook's greaser saw him—Singin Sam, he saw him. The axe caught his eye. He was out on the ice fishin through a hole—with Sabael! An after that he was down there nearly ever week.

Wal, one night—now this is gettin end a February—one night the cook come in. She said Sabael's gone. Gone least a week. His fire was out. The ashes had frost on em.

So we asked Savree. He said didn't know. They sent a party after him, the sheriff an some others. But they said couldn't find him. No tracks.

Then that wind come down the lake, makin screams'n'hollers. We heered em lots a years a course. But they was, they had a way to em now. Over'n'over, same thing.

First there was a big rip. Like somebody tore up the ice. Then howlin. Like all them wolves Sabael had hangin round. Then someone yellin, "Gold! Gold!" We heered it. All of us heered it. Then a big crack'n'a scream.

Wal, Savree looked up, an his eyes was like two cigar holes burned in a blanket.

That callin kept up ever night. It was up one end the lake, down nuther. An Savree took ta actin queer. One night he run out there, commenced yellin. Wahnt a soul out there. Jest the moon an that callin. "Gold! Gold!" Like it was movin. Movin under the ice. Like it was tryin ta get out.

It stopped real quick when the ice broke up. An a week after, the sheriff rides in. The cook said he was probly lookin ta see if we had deer meat. But there wahnt nuthin but salt pork' n'beans.

We was bunked in here. A card game was goin. Not much else. I said ta Nick, somethin don't feel right.

All ta once the sheriff breaks in. He shuts the door. He bars it. An he says Sabael floated down the inlet. His head was smashed in. He said we knew who done it. "Out with it!" he says.

Wal, we swore up'n'down we didn't know. We cursed the man done it. We stamped around. But the sheriff stood. He said it was one a us.

Now ya don't like ta think bad of a shanty mate. But we was all looking at Savree, a-layin on that bunk, next his axe.

"Out with it!" the sheriff says. "Which a ya done it?"

"I keel heem! I keel heem!" Savree tumbles down. "But he leeve! In ice. He call." They put the bracelets on him. "He have monee. He old."

He told some story bout a girl he loved. How the gold was so's he could marry her. Cause her pa turned him out. "So! Where's the gold?"

He never told. Never told. Not where his own was, neither. We figgered he hid em same place. An they took him up to a convict camp.

There got ta be a story goin. Singin Sam made a song of it. Bout how Savree hid the gold in a tree. An how the tree grew up round it. An how one day a chopper bit inta that tree. An out comes a sack a gold! Fallin like snow! An how we put on a time at the Crick. An we all made a verse bout what we done. An some a that I don't care ta repeat.

That was a long time ago.

Oh! Did we hunt fer that gold. Folks're still huntin for it.

They tell me the Company's movin out. But I bet Sabael still be here. Howlin fer his gold. "Gold! Gold!" An I bet ya still hear Savree clompin down the hill with that axe in his hand.

I wouldn't go out there. Not tanight. Not if I was you.

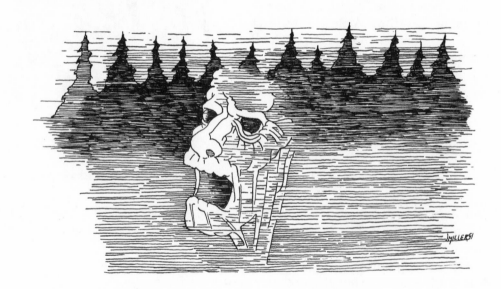

A BOAT RIDE WITH MITCHELL SABATTIS

Location: the outlet of Long Lake, c. 1844

Source: Joel T. Headley, *The Adirondack or, Life in the Woods* (1849)

Mitchell Sabattis, a St. Francis Indian, was one of the legendary Long Lake guides. Headley was a celebrated writer of travel and history books.

Further reading: Philip G. Terrie, "Introduction," *The Adirondack or, Life in the Woods*, reprint ed. (1982), 5-22

We seemed to move by invisible hands. I knelt in the bow. Mitchell sat in the stern. He was still as a statue.

I knew we were moving only when I looked down and saw the reflections of stars passing beneath us. Though I strained every nerve, I never once heard the paddle, not even a drop of water.

Mysteriously we turned and entered a channel. The banks closed in dense black. We moved through a world of eerie shadows. Tufts rose from the water and grew to gigantic size as we passed. Little bays and rocky points took on grotesque shapes.

Silence. Then the far-off scream of a loon.

We glided over a constellation. We crossed the shadow of a pine.

We continued for a mile, then, mysteriously, we turned again and entered what seemed to be a cove. Or was it the mouth of a cave? Nothing was clear. I leaned forward, but the more I looked, the more confused I was.

Gradually the shapes began receding. They were drawing away. Was the whole scene a dream? Was it mist dissolving? I looked below me. The stars, too, were melting away.

Then I realized what it was. Mitchell had reversed direction! He was drawing us backwards. But I had felt nothing, heard not a sound. Never before had I witnessed such skill with a boat.

AMELIA MURRAY'S ADIRONDACK TREK

for Joan Payne

Location: Essex, Franklin, Hamilton, Herkimer, and Oneida Counties, 1855

Source: Amelia M. Murray, *Letters from the United States, Cuba and Canada* (1856)

"What Happened on My Adirondack Vacation" is a story all visitors love to tell. Amelia Murray was sixty years old at the time of her journey. She had come from England, where she was Maid of Honor to Queen Victoria and an amateur artist and botanist. In July of 1855 New York Governor Seymour and his wife accompanied her to Trenton Falls north of Utica, and in September the Governor took her on a nine-day trip through the mountains, following the classic canoe route that has been used by thousands of travelers from Indian times to the present.

Thursday, September 12

We reached the Saranac Lake about an hour after dark, conveyed by buckboards and wagons. It was much too civilized a means of transportation, but from here we go on by boat or on foot and hope to travel more than a hundred miles with packs on our backs and staffs in our hands. One cannot imagine how delightful it will be.

Our drive from Elizabethtown to this place was about thirty-two miles. The road was rough but practicable by walking up the steepest parts. We passed through fine passes and grand mountains. I made a sketch in which Tahawus was included. And on our way we picked a variety of wild fruits — blackberries, huckleberries, cherries — and, above all, a little red plum. It is rather hard and tart. The guides said it was quite useless. But I thought it would make a good plum pudding. So I picked enough for that purpose.

It was quite dark for an hour before we reached Baker's, this last house of reception. Once we nearly made our way into a shed instead of following the road. But after backing out, our resting place was soon reached.

We thought ourselves unhappy at sleeping indoors, though it was three to a room, and the walls are only rough boards. However, this will be the last time for some days we shall have any other canopy than heaven over our heads (and, of course, the small tent which is to be carried with us.)

Friday, September 13

Our head guide, Mr. Moody, rowed the boat. I had a most comfortable seat of cloaks and cushions and the company of Governor Seymour. His niece, Miss Monroe, together with Mr. Hunt, were conducted in another boat by a fine youth of nineteen, who goes by the curious name of "Prince Albert." It is believed he was so christened at two years of age. But he looked shy and annoyed when asked about it. And the baggage came along in a boat behind.

The weather was perfect. We glided on water as smooth as glass, passing by lovely islands and fine rocks. For the first time I saw the loon and heard its wild cry — more resembling a mocking laugh than anything else. I could have fancied it saying, "You intruders! You will have enough of this before you are done!" Ah, but you wait! We will be the victors here! A fine eagle soared over our heads and ravens also.

At the first rapids we disembarked that the men might carry and push their boats through. I sketched during this operation. Then we proceeded to a small round lake set among mountains.

And now we had a portage. Each man carried a boat upon his head — rather curious looking I must say. Miss Monroe and I filled my Scotch plaid with baskets and bundles and bore it between us. The distance was short, but it was above an hour before we were afloat again, this time in the Upper Saranac.

Finally we chose a spot to camp. The guides built up a great log fire, and I gathered brush and pine cones to help the blaze. We also broke off small branches of the hemlock tree, which in this country makes the sweetest and best foundation for an Alpine bed. It's sweeter than, though not quite so pretty, as our heather. Over this the Governor spread a thin oilskin. My air cushions were most valuable. We puffed them up, and with these and my leather bag as a bolster, large plaids and felt coverings — and Miss Monroe's black and scarlet shawl as a curtain of division — we two ladies and gentlemen slept soundly, after making a hearty supper of trout and potatoes.

I had brought along a dozen lemons, aware that when no milk can be had, the juice makes an excellent addition to tea. This plan was unamimously approved. Even the guides were pleased. (In the forest, of course, all fare is common potluck.) "It aint bad," they said. This implies almost as high praise as, "It won't hurt ya." And that, in these parts, is the acme.

I also concocted my pudding — with the wild plums (deprived of their stones, of course). I added biscuit, brown sugar, a little butter, and some water. But alas, the plums were rather more hard and acid than I thought. Many, many hours stewing was required. Indeed, the dish was not produced until breakfast the next day. And then it tasted like no more than boiled wood.

One of the boats was turned upside down for our table. Our candlestick was a large potato placed on a tin pail inverted.

The guides slept outside, close about our little tent. About half-past two, according to a common habit in these parts, we all roused up for half an hour to replenish the fire and attend to other necessities. I removed my stew to a little fire of its own that it might not get all stewed away before morning. We then composed ourselves as before and had comfortable naps till daylight.

During the night I heard a most dreadful noise. I called to Moody. I thought it might be a wolf. But he assured me it was only a screech owl.

Saturday, September 14

Preparations for breakfast began at five o'clock: frying pork, boiling trout and potatoes and water for tea. At the last the smaller trout were fried in the same pan with the pork gravy — which makes an excellent dish. Afterwards we ladies went down to the lake to arrange ourselves. We had to balance in one of the boats to use our toothbrushes.

While the guides were packing up and preparing to undertake the portage to Stony Creek, I made a sketch and caught one of them in the act of carrying the boat with his head concealed underneath — rather like some nondescript shellfish.

But before we started, the Governor and Mr. Hunt hung a small mirror of Mary's on a tree limb and very composedly shaved themselves. It was a most affecting scene, but modesty prevented me from sketching it.

The guides took the boats upon their heads, and after two

MR. MOODY

returns had transported all the baggage the rest of the party could not carry. We now reached Otter's Creek and the Raquette River, where there was such good fishing that a long pause ensued. I landed to sketch the scenery and was so much absorbed as to leave my parasol in a bush. We had to row back a half mile for its recovery.

At Raquette Falls we had a mile and a half of excrutiating portage. The signs of a trail were barely visible. Gigantic trees crossed our path, sometimes every twenty yards. Deep bogs and slippery rocks impeded us. Each of us struggled on as best he or she could. Often we had to retrace our steps or seek a blazed tree before we could find our way. When Mr. Seymour had conveyed his load above the falls, he kindly returned to relieve me of whatever basket or bundle I was still able to carry. And so, at last, we reached our second camping place.

Our tent was pitched at the edge of the river. A bright fire was lit, and another for cooking near our boat table. The largest trout were boiled and the smaller ones fried with potatoes. Tea-lemonade was our beverage.

Afterwards we played a game of whist with a not very clean pack of cards procured from one of the guides. Then we arranged ourselves as on the night before and slept soundly till one o'clock, when the fires were stirred up. Then we napped again till morning. This night not a single sound disturbed our slumber save the rippling water at our feet.

Sunday, September 15

I awoke at six o'clock to a gentle rain pattering upon the trees. But it was only "the pride of the morning," just enough to make us more sensible of the blessing of fine weather.

For our dressing room Miss Monroe selected a sheltered rocky nook a little ways back. There we bathed with a luxury of towels and used our combs and toothbrushes—and Miss Monroe's mirror hung upon the lowest branch of a hemlock.

We came forth arrayed in cleanliness. Its opposite is at times picturesque but not comfortable. On the whole I was impressed by the tidy habits of our three guides. They omitted no opportunity for using the fresh water to wash away impurities and never left cup or platter in a soiled state if they could help it. This smartening-up of the individual woman was all that marked our Sunday morning, for no Sabbath rest can be set aside for travelers in the bush.

The approach to Long Lake was so thickly covered with lily pads and other plants, it seemed we were making our way across a watery meadow. When we reached the lake, our guides had to row fourteen miles against the wind. We saw cabins along the shore. Once a boy of ten paddled his little canoe towards us, and when we asked if many people lived there, he said, "There's the baby and some more." What a charming answer!

Tonight we camped behind a rocky knoll.

Monday, September 16

Today we had two or three difficult and fatiguing portages. I awoke to some fine rain again, but with the aid of my large umbrella I did not miss a sketch of our camp. And the palmetto fly-flapper I had brought from Mobile, Alabama, proved of great use in frightening away mosquitos.

But it was muddy walking and we were thoroughly bespattered. However, Jamie McClelland consoled us by the assurance he had seen women looking much worse. There were moose tracks at the edge of the stream, plenty of signs of deer, one or two solitary crane, and a bald eagle.

Alas, the men determined to ride through the last rapids, now touching one rock, now fast upon another. I did not find this adventure amusing. And in all the excitement I lost hold of my palmetto fly-flapper.

I observed a yellow sunset as we rowed up Raquette Lake with heaped-up clouds in the south. The suspicion crossed my mind we were in for stormy weather. And indeed, growling thunder, vivid lightning, and a pouring rain disturbed our slumbers—not to mention that our hemlock beds became rather damp.

Tuesday, September 17

There was another violent storm this morning, so any intention of striking our tent was abandoned. Instead, the guides turned it so as to face the fire and accommodate it to the change of wind. They had stowed themselves under the boats during the night, and this appeared to have sheltered them more completely than our tent did us.

During this rainy pause in our wanderings I could not help being struck by the picturesque appearance inside our tent. There we were seated upon the ground, the rain drumming over our heads, with pans of tea and plates of tin; with air cushions, plaids, and felts scattered about; also sketch books, flower presses, books and maps; a tin case containing our store of grocery, and a huge basket full of biscuits. There was a hammer ensconced among bunches of berries; tallow candles, towels, hats and bonnets, and other items of attire, with touches of scarlet and blue—all of it lit up by the glow of the fire outside. It would have made a painting even for Gerard Dow!

No colds were caught, and the weather cleared in the afternoon.

Wednesday, September 18

We embarked again in high spirits. And we ate Mr. Moody's partridge for breakfast. It proved excellent. And I did not omit to sketch the encampment before we left.

The weather had turned colder, and as we rowed up Raquette Lake, a slight snowstorm overtook us. But it was soon over. The lake was beautiful with numerous bays and islands and blue mountains rising in the distance.

We passed through a narrow channel for some way, then disembarked for a portage to the eighth lake of the Fulton Chain, where lakes of differing magnitude are strung upon the Moose river. On the seventh lake we observed a tempting rocky promontory, and as the sun was getting low, we decided to land on a pretty beach behind it.

We all enjoyed this camp particularly. I made a can of excellent portable soup, a provision we had tried before with some success. But this time I added arrowroot, an onion, potatoes, two or three spoonfuls of sweet wine, and several biscuits. It was generally agreed this mixture "wouldn't kill anybody." Indeed! Anywhere else it would have been considered an excellent soup.

I strongly recommend London Portable Soup to all travelers in the bush. Although I had brought mine and the arrowroot from England more than a year ago, they were still in good preservation. I also advise you to take lemons and a good store of sugar, both brown and white.

We had a bright moon this night. Some hunters and fishermen were on the lake, and from the latter we procured trout.

Thursday, September 19

It was misty this morning, but the mountaintops soon peaked out. We passed from one lake to another, sometimes by outlets so narrow we had difficulty in finding them. Once our boatmen had to row up and down a considerable distance before a swampy-looking egress was discovered.

This led us into a pretty winding creek, and another short portage brought us below the falls of the Moose River. Here the Governor walked ahead to make some arrangements at Arnold's farm, while we ladies had a pleasant row in charge of Mr. Moody and Jamie McClelland and saw canvasback ducks in the river.

At Arnold's farm we expected to find horses, but owing to our delay in the rain storm, the horses had been sent off to bring up some gentlemen from Brown's Tract. So, pedestrianism was our only recourse. Mrs. Arnold was furious. She all but tried to detain us by force. She declared we could not possibly get through. She would soon see us back. Ah, but we felt the importance of determination. And besides, by now we were far too experienced gypsies to fear camping out.

For a mile we did have a pleasant walk. But then commenced a series of bog holes. With few and short intervals we had to scramble through them for sixteen miles. The worst of it was that when night closed in we could not find a dry spot to pitch our tent. Finally we sent Jamie on, and he brought back the news he had found a little knoll above the bogs.

Dark as it was I reached this spot with only an occasional flounder in the mud. Jamie cut down a birch of considerable size and built up a fire, which I assisted in lighting by breaking off brush from the surrounding bush. Before long Mr. Seymour and the other guides joined us. They were astonished how we had ever got through the places which had nearly swamped them. What did I tell you about our being experienced gypsies? The tent was raised and soon a fire blazed ready for cooking.

Oh, but we did have one misfortune. Poor young Prince Albert lay on the ground agonized and quite useless. We gave him what comfort we could, and I administered camphor, which soothed the pain and enabled him to sleep. Mr. Moody told me he knew the value of camphor and seldom went into the forest without it.

I forgot to mention a curious scene at Arnold's farm. When we went in, we found Mrs. Arnold and six daughters. These girls, aged twelve to twenty, were placed in a row against one wall of the shanty. They looked at me with such astonishment I was puzzled to account for it. Finally, Mrs. Arnold informed me they had never before seen a woman other than herself. I could not get a single word from them.

Friday, September 20

There was sufficient portable soup and arrowroot to make a good warm mess for breakfast. And so nourishing is it that with the exception of half a biscuit and some water, I got on upon only this until we reached Boonville after nine in the evening.

But before we left, we parted from our three guides, who had conducted themselves so excellently throughout our difficulties. Jamie, who is Canadian, was going back to take his wife of nineteen to his father's house near Montreal. (He has been married to her for four years.)

Mr. Seymour must always be considered a brave man to have undertaken to conduct us alone on that last day's tramp. But happily he had never passed through this track before and was not aware of what he undertook.

Our path was a road cut through the wilderness some fifty years ago. Planks had been laid down and corduroy bridges built. But as no settlement followed, all this was left to rot. It made bad worse. I cannot imagine anywhere a track so difficult to get over as that through which we labored for ten consecutive hours. But Mr. Seymour's patience and good humor never gave way. Putting off the packages from his own back, he extricated now one lady, now another from a boggy fix.

I shall never forget the astonishment of Mr. Stephens (of yachting fame) when on horseback with another gentleman and guides, he met us crawling out of the bush. They had four horses, and one was secured for me. It was not easy to keep my seat upon a man's saddle, but I was immediately aware of the benefit of being carried by some agency other than my own feet.

We crossed the Moose River again, and another two hours brought us to a clearing where a small wagon was procured. Rough it was, but still a wagon. It took us to a small hotel in Boonville. After a night's rest we went on by coach and cars to Utica, where just two months before we had come to view Trenton Falls. But there was no such excursion on this occasion. Indeed, three days were required to recruit repose myself.

OLD MOUNTAIN PHELPS

Location: Keene Valley and the High Peaks, Essex County, 1870s

Source: Charles Dudley Warner, *In the Wilderness* (1876)

Warner (1829-1900) lived in Hartford, Connecticut, where he was a newspaper editor, travel writer, humorist, and champion of American literature.

Also from Warner: "A-Hunting of the Deer," 105; "How I Got a Bear," 123

Further reading: *The Complete Writings of Charles Dudley Warner* (1904); Annie A. Fields, *Charles Dudley Warner* (1904)

He was a true citizen of the wilderness. Thoreau would have liked him. He knew every foot of the forest, all woodcraft, all signs of the weather. He was fisherman and hunter, a comrade of sportsmen and explorers.

From the first, visitors pronounced him the best guide in the region. But he exercised his profession reluctantly for those who had no love of the woods. It was a waste of his time to guide flippant young men and giddy girls who made a lark of the expedition. "You can't git boys ta take any kind a notice a scenery. I aint seen a boy once take a second look at a sunset."

He told of some ladies he once led to the top of Marcy. "Mt. Mercy" is what he called it. It was the chief mountain of the globe as far as he was concerned.

When he and his ladies stood at last on the rocky summit, the deep valleys winding below them, the lakes sparkling here and there like bits of broken mirror—the whole prospect from horizon to horizon a tumultuous sea of billows turned to stone —his ladies turned to each other and began talking.

Phelps's eyes popped as he recalled the scene. He turned in the trail. His voice rose to a shriek. "There they was, right front a the greatest sight they ever seen, talkin bout the fashions! I was half a mind ta come down an leave em there!"

His own clothes seemed put on him once and for all—like the bark of a tree. In fact he looked like he'd just come out of the ground. "Soap's a thing I aint no kind a use for. Aint no use in the woods when ya got soap on."

His hat was limp and frayed. His hair sprang out the top like a fern. His legs were bowed. The beard was cut only enough to make room for a mouth.

He'd come from Vermont, built a log house near a brook, planted apple trees, and reared a family. But he had no ambitions to civilize the wilderness. Quite the contrary. His most characteristic pose was sitting on a log with a short pipe in his mouth. His neighbors called him lazy, but if ever a man was born to sit on a log, it was old Phelps.

I recall one Indian summer morning when a party of us found him on his doorstep, smoking a pipe. He seemed quite in harmony with the day. We had to stand there a full minute before he took note of us.

"See that tree?" He pointed his pipe towards a maple near the brook. "I ben watchin that tree—all mornin. Now there aint ben a breath a wind. But all mornin them leaves a ben fallin. Fallin straight down. An lyin like ya see em." The leaves lay about the base like a discarded robe. "An now it's pretty much bare . . . Wal, I s'pose his hour was come." He sat a while longer. "Now I want ya to see my golden city."

His "golden city"?

He led the way to an outlook. Below us was a vast assemblage of birches blazing in color. "There tis. My golden city." Then he took out his pipe and sat.

His features were small and surprisingly delicate—small gray eyes set close together, a childlike mouth, hands and feet of an aristocratic smallness. And there was an internal fineness as well. Not the artificial fineness of the drawing room, but the fineness of a man who has grown up in the company of mountains and forests and wild animals.

I remember our first journey to Lower Ausable Lake. It was a tedious march through the forest, but then, suddenly, the lake broke upon our vision—low lying, silver, surrounded by rock precipices. He made no outward response to our burst of admiration. but a quiet gleam in his eye showed the pleasure our appreciation gave him. It was as if a friend had been praised, a dear friend about whom he was reluctant to say much himself but well pleased to have others admire.

And when we went on to the Upper Lake and wanted to build our lean-to on the

south shore—so we might have a full view of the Gothics—to our surprise old Phelps opposed us. He said he preferred camping on the north shore.

It was a pleasant place, but it had no particular view. To see the mountains we would have to row out on the lake. We wanted them always before our eyes—at sunrise and sunset, and in the blaze of noon. No. Phelps thought otherwise. "Wal, now, I calate them Gothics aint the kind a scenery ya wanna hog down!"

His voice invariably startled the newcomer. Already high-pitched, it rose easily into the shrillest falsetto. It was clearly audible in thunder storms and above the roar of rapids. When arguing it rose even higher. There was an eeriness when you heard it in the depths of the woods, quavering aloft.

Yet it also had a softer ring. One day, climbing up the Balcony, he saw a little flower in the crevice of a rock. He was unusually slow that day, poking everywhere. Then he came upon a tiny flower, perfectly formed, which he cradled between two fingers. His voice was completely changed. "It looks as if the Creator put somethin here just ta look at Himself."

One lady he took to Chapel Pond found the place disappointing. She remarked on how tame it was. His only reply "Ay-uh. Ay-uh. It lies here just where it was born."

He didn't care much for what he called "the religion of ceremony." Indeed, Keene Valley had a reputation for not ripening Christians any more successfully than it ripened corn. For many years I counted only one Bible Christian, though others said there were three.

Nevertheless, Phelps often came to our Bible classes. We held them outdoors with each member choosing a site in turn. We'd be working our way through the day's lesson when all of a sudden old Phelps'd pipe up from a tree where he was leaning. "I ben thinkin bout that word, that word, God's word being written on the heart. An I ben askin myself just how that writin on the heart's ta be done. Wal, I'll tell ya.

"Cause last week we had a photo-grapher. An I watched him. What ya do is ya set that thing in position, and the sun takes the picture. So if ya want that writin on yer heart, what ya do is, ya put yer heart in position, an God does the writin."

One year they had a religious revival in Keene Valley. "That man began back there at creation an just preached right along on down. He didn't say nuthin. He was just gettin up some kind a literary fix-up."

But the result was a number of young converts. "Wal now, Jimmy, ya kindled a pretty good fire there with light wood. That's what we do of a dark night. So's we can go out'n'find the solid wood. So Jimmy, you go on out there now an put on yer solid wood.''

Someone asked where we'd go the next day. "Wal, I calerate, if they rig up the caleration they calerate on, we'll go ta the Boreas." And starting out for the tramp, he'd ask if we wanted a "regler walk" or a "random scoot."

When he got tangled in brush, he looked like a wizard—axe in hand, peering this way and that, a canvas sack on his shoulder. "There aint no specalation there!" And if the way became altogether inscrutable: "This here's a regler random scoot of a rigmarole!"

In later years he talked more than he worked. Some of his critics even went so far as to call him a fraud. But probably they'd have said the same thing about Socrates. No doubt he went gabbing about Athens with little care for supper. And no doubt he cooked no better than old Phelps.

And there were better trappers, better hunters. But Orson Phelps loved the mountains, loved them like no other. He alone climbed them solely for the prospect. He alone took pleasure in the seasons and enjoyed the woods for themselves.

I remember our last climb up Marcy. He led a party of us to the top by the way he'd bushed out. It was some time since he visited his mountain, and as the rest of us grew weary of the forest, he pushed on with the eagerness of a lover going to a rendezvous.

Along the foot of the mountain we crossed a stream. He stooped over and whispered to it. "So, little brook, do we meet again?" And when we emerged at last on the summit, above the last ragged fringe of vegetation, I saw him hurry ahead and cast himself on the ground. "I'm with you again!"

The mountaintop was swept by a fierce wind that day. Occasionally it was lost in a damp cloud. Exhausted by the climb and shivering in the cold, some of the party wanted a fire kindled and tea made. They thought this the guide's business. But old

Phelps had withdrawn himself quite apart. He sat wrapped in a blanket, his back to a rock, still and silent, gazing out over that wilderness of peaks. I think some of the boys finally got a fire started.

On our way down we went west toward Avalanche and Colden and crossed another stream. "Wal now, here's little Miss Opalescent!"

"Mr. Phelps, why don't you call her Mr. Opalescent?"

"Cause she's . . . she's too pretty."

He had no more faculty for acquiring property than a deer. But he held in his heart more of what makes these mountains special than all his neighbors put together. "Ta have hours such as I did in these moun'ns—Ya know, these moun'ns ta me are like a man's farm is ta him—An with company the likes a Dr. Buchnell and Dr. Shaw and Mr. Twichell, an, an—An others I could name—That's ben worth more ta me than all the money—than alllll the money—the world could give."

SONNY'S COAT

Location: Buck Mountain, Warren County, 1890s
Source: Jeanne Robert Foster, *Neighbors of Yesterday* (1916)
Also from Foster: "The Last Tarrin'n'Featherin," 85; "The Lumberjack's Tale," 49; Nance's Baby," 35; "The Old Church," 133

Out past the tannery, up an old lumber road, round the last turn, was the strangest kind of house. It was chinked against a ledge where the creek comes down off Buck Mountain. It was made of old boards, every shade of gray and brown with patches of moss. The roof was gray, made of bark shingles. The rafters were always wet. The granite dooryard was strewn with rocks.

You couldn't see it at first. Then the door opened and things stirred that looked like shreds of bark. And some smoke up top told you someone lived there. It was Ben Hewitt and his wife.

"I'll tell ya what lightnin's made of," he'd say. "A ball burst right here'n the yard. Right there. It was full of shingle nails an tin an things. An bolts. An Lord knows the mess."

He didn't like doctors.

"Them durn fool doctors! They give ya devil's pills. There's lungweed when ya git dartin pains. An yer a fool if ya don't take hemlock sweats fer fever. An plant'n leaves. I cured a cancer once with plant'n leaves."

Somehow word got around that old Ben was a miser. They said he kept his pension money in the house. One stormy night thugs broke in. They gagged his wife and trussed her in the corner like a sack.

Ben wouldn't tell where the money was. They said they'd burn his feet if he didn't tell. But he wouldn't. So they opened the stove door. They carried him over, and they shoved his feet in.

The storm hid his cries. He passed out. They thought he was dead. He couldn't walk for a year.

I asked him why, why he did it.

"Go ahind that stair door and bring me Sonny's coat."

It was Union blue, old, faded, patched. The straps were rusting.

"It's Sonny's coat. In here's where my money is."

He reached deep in a pocket and brought out a few coins.

"Ever time I git a coin I think a him. How he crawled over an caught my boot an pulled hisself up an grinned. An called me papa.

"He had yella hair. An blue eyes, bright blue eyes.

"That crick outside, it makes a sound like Sonny's laugh. I heered it one day. I bent down ta git a drink an I heered Sonny's laugh. So I built the house here.

"When I go out there, I never know when I'll hear Sonny's laugh."

"He went to war?"

"Ay-uh. He went'n'volunteered. I told him no. He was jest a boy. Sonny was fifteen. But he wouldn't listen. He had ta go with me.

"One night at Freddysburg we was layin ahind some sod. He was tired a all that waitin. He wanted ta git up an fight the rebs.

"That's what war is. Waitin an dyin.

"So they dared him. 'Git up an wave yer hat!'

"They was jest boys fightin the war. Sonny was fifteen.

"Wal, he stood up an waved his hat. An them Tennessee rebs drew a bead on him. He never made a sound.

"When he stood up, I . . . I called him a name. It's the last thing he ever heered from his pa. I never got ta tell him . . .

"This pocket's tore a dozen time. I always mend it.

"Robbers aint gonna lay hands on Sonny's coat. It's gonna lay by me in my coffin."

MITCHELL SABATTIS' PROMISE

Location: Long Lake, Newcomb, and Burlington, 1846-47

Source: L. E. Chittenden, *Personal Reminiscences, Including Lincoln and Others, 1840-1890* (1893)

At the time of this story Chittenden was twenty-four and at the start of a brilliant career in banking and politics. He helped organize the Free Soil party, which eventually became the Republican party, and he served President Lincoln as a treasury official. Mitchell Sabattis was one of the legendary Long Lake guides.

Mitchell was head guide the first time I made up a camping party. And what a performance!

One night I shot a deer—and heard it run off. I was furious with myself, but Mitchell was unconcerned. He said the deer was wounded and would soon die. How could he tell? By the sound of the deer running. He bent over, and in a pile of leaves he found a drop of blood. By lanternlight! He tracked that deer up the mountain for a mile, found where it died, and brought it back—all by lanternlight. He could

handle a canoe as silently as a ghost. He knew where
trout were hiding, and, more important, he knew the
exact day and hour when they would rise to the bait.

I spent my last night at his home in Newcomb. He
and his wife seemed depressed. He hardly touched his
food. Finally his wife told me there was a mortgage on
their farm. It would be sold in four weeks. She learned
this while he was away with me. Where would they go?
They had five children.

And there was more. Mitchell drank. His wife said
he was a good husband and a good father, but when he
drank he went mad. I looked at Mitchell. He sat stone-
faced as she sobbed. If the farm was sold, she knew
he'd get worse.

Next morning while the horses were waiting, I asked
him, "Mitchell, what would you give if someone
bought your mortgage and gave you time to pay it?"
He said if Bessie and the children could keep the
house, he'd give his life.

I told him I was going to Elizabethtown. I would
buy the mortgage. The house would not be sold.
But I wanted a promise from him. "Next summer I
want you to meet me at Bartlett's. If you can tell me
you've had no liquor since you last saw me, you won't
have to worry about the mortgage." Instantly he
promised. "Mitchell, as long as you keep your promise, your wife and children will have a home." He
rose from his chair. He looked every inch the chief.

His wife spoke through tears. She knew he'd keep
his promise. He was proud. He never broke his word.
She was the happiest woman alive.

Some months went by. One night in February,
in Burlington, an hour or so before supper, I
was sitting by the window watching the
snow when a long sleigh came up the
street. It was a huge box five feet
high and perhaps eight feet long. It
was drawn by two horses. The run-
ners were crooks cut from tree roots.
The sides were rough boards sup-
ported by stakes.

MITCHELL SABATTIS

The driver walked beside the horses. He was wrapped in bearskin. He stopped almost in front of my window. I thought he must be lost, but when I went out, I heard my name.

"Mr. Chittenden."

"Wha—Mitchell? Mitchell Sabattis?"

"This big town, Mr. Chittenden. Many house."

"But why are you here? It's a hundred and fifty miles from Newcomb!"

"Bessie say come. No work now. She say bring game."

I took him to a stable where his load was put under lock and key. He expected to stay with the horses, but of course I took him home.

He was very neat and courtly. I can still see the clear skin, the clear eyes. Obviously he'd kept his word. When food was served, he ate with impeccable manners. He made a great impression on the household.

It seems there'd been a complete turnaround. He'd worked all summer and fall as a guide. He killed more deer than ever before, and he got good prices. He paid off all his small debts and saved a hundred dollars. Bessie said he should bring the money to me, and she thought I'd like a little game. So he built the sled, borrowed two horses, made up the load, and walked to Crown Point. From there he made his way up the lake to Burlington. It took him five days.

Next morning I went to see his "little load of game."

There were hind quarters of twenty-five deer wrapped in their skins. There were two bear dressed and returned to their skins. A magnificent panther skin—measuring nine feet—with the head and claws attached. Half a dozen skins of pine marten, a hundred pounds of brook trout, ten dozen grouse dressed and braided. Mink and fox skins, smaller game. It was magnificent.

I took what I could use. He would accept no money from me, but my butcher paid handsomely for the rest. Now he had more than enough to pay the mortgage. But I wasn't ready to lose my hold on him.

He talked about adding two rooms on the house so Bessie could keep boarders in the summer. It was the perfect solution. He paid me the interest and part of the principal on the mortgage and spent the rest on furniture for the new rooms and on presents for Bessie and the children.

And he kept his promise. He never drank again. He became a leader in the Methodist church in Long Lake. His wife kept a popular boarding house. Two of his sons fought in the war, and both came back unharmed. No doubt it was the skills Mitchell taught them in the woods that saved their lives. His daughters married well.

He died at eighty-four, full of years and honor. In my estimation Mitchell Sabattis was the noblest work of God—an honest man.

HITCH-UP, MATILDA!

for the old gang at Hemlock Hall

Location: Lake Placid and the High Peaks, Essex County, 1868
Source: Seneca Ray Stoddard, *The Adirondacks: Illustrated* (1874)
Stoddard (1844-1917), the Adirondacks' first photographer, also gave the region its first travel guide. In it he provided timetables, routes, distances, prices, and also stories. This one, told to Stoddard by William B. Nye, has become the Adirondacks' best known hikers' folktale.
Further reading: Maitland De Sormo, *Seneca Ray Stoddard, Versatile Camera-Artist* (1972).

They was a party a three stayin at Nash's — Mr. an Mrs. Fieldin. They come from down the Hudson somewheres. An they brung their niece, Dolly, Seventeen she was. Real friendly. Talked ta anyone. Pretty. Gold hair.

Wal, they ben settin on the porch there at Nash's, lookin at the scenery. Till one day they got the notion ta go in there. On account a that niece, I s'pose. Give her somethin ta do. Cause she looked ta me like she had somethin on her mind more'n listen ta them ladies. An they asked if I'd guide em.

So I took some carrots'n'tates up ta Colden, hid em away. They thought a goin in through Indian Pass an up Marcy an come out Avalanche Pass. I cut some wood. Have it ready for em.

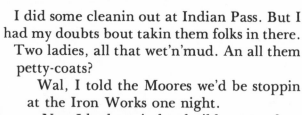

BILL NYE

I did some cleanin out at Indian Pass. But I had my doubts bout takin them folks in there. Two ladies, all that wet'n'mud. An all them petty-coats?

Wal, I told the Moores we'd be stoppin at the Iron Works one night.

Now I had a mind ta build em a raft at Avalanche Lake. Have it ready for em. But it was rainin—

I ought'n ta say this—An I don wan it gettin out.

Course when they's a party I'm guidin, it can rain turnips. Don mind me. Jus so's my party's okay. Don mind me. Wal, cept when a city man comes up an tells me how ta dress out a deer. But when I'm out, jus me, an it rains, rains like that —wal, that's time ta head out. Now snow, snow don mind me. But rain . . .

So, I come out. Wal, I wahnt thinkin. I thought they was time ta build em a raft if we left Colden early. An they can set a piece, look at the scenery. Wal, I say it again, I wahnt thinkin.

Now seems the ladies there at Nash's was tellin Mrs. Fieldin she'll catch her death a cold goin in there. Probly break a leg. She won't last a hour.

Wal, Mr. Fieldin hears em say it. So he says mebby they ought'n ta go. Or mebby they just go partway. Or mebby we take Dolly an leave that Misses home. But nex day he says no, they'll go. An nex night he says no, they won't.

Wal, that's when Mrs. Fieldin put her word in. She says she's goin. Now I was there. I heered her say it. She says she's goin if he goes er not. An she had a couple things ta say ta Mr. Fieldin. So two days after, we went.

An them two days Dolly was over me! Showin me her shoes she was gonna wear. An her . . . hat.

Wal, they was all carryin their shoes fore the end a that day. It was blacker'n a bear's belly fore we got ta the Iron Works.

When it come dark, I tole em I'll build em a camp. But Mrs. Fieldin says no. "Lead on!" she says. An that's a woman when her mind's made up, there aint no talkin. So four mile we're crawlin over rocks, in'n'out a mud. All the way by torchlight. You oughta seen Mr. Fieldin. He looked like a rat gettin hit by a hawk.

Mrs. Moore had venson-biscuits for us, bless her heart.

Now nex day wahnt bad. Gettin ta Colden. Then up Marcy'n'back. But wahnt nuthin get them folks out a bed the last day. I whistled. I banged the pots. Not a sound in there till after eight. So we got a late start.

An a course Dolly had ta fix herself. Lord knows she didn't need it! She knew it, too. I tell ya, a gal like that makes ya think . . . things. But I'm too old a dog fer that.

So we get up ta Avalanche, an there aint no time ta build a raft. Food's gettin short. So I tole em I'll carry em down the lake ta save time. I showed em where the shelf is, how deep it is. Mrs. Fieldin put her hand in the water. I tole em I carried a man from Masschuset weighed a hundred-eighty pound.

So Mr. Fieldin says, "Wal, Matilda, will ya"—Oh, cause that was her name, Matilda. He says, "Matilda, will ya be carried er do ya wanna wait'n'make a raft?"

So she looks me over, feels the water. An she says, "Wal, if Mr. Nye says he can do it, I'll be carried. Ta save time." But she didn't say it too nice.

Then Dolly giggles, an she says, "If Auntie Matilda can do it, so can I!" An she giggles some more, way them gals do. She talked like it wahnt nuthin more ta her ridin me'n ridin a horse.

But I'm thinkin, what kind a business is this? Wadda my gonna say when George an Pete an Ed Smith an Ed Kenney, when they hear I ben totin women round my neck? An their petty-coats in my face? An one of em *seventeen*?

Wal, all I can say is, it was my duty. But I kep quiet about it. Never said a word.

Till Pete Aldridge heard it. I don know where Pete heard it. Them ladies never said it. Leastways not around me. I aint never found out where Pete heard it.

Wal, first I wade long the wall, make sure it's okay. Ya know how rocks fall in there, get piled up. Now one place was a lot deeper'n I recalled. Clear up ta my arm. But keepin close by the wall I got through. Course I didn't have nuthin on me but a pack.

I get back and Mr. Fieldin says, "Okay, Matilda, you go first. Ladies first."

Wal, she gives me a look. Course I'm standin there drippin wet. An she says, "No." She don see how I'm gonna get cross there an

THE IRON WORKS

keep her outta the water. She says, "You go first." And he says, "Matilda, it's only polite ladies go first." So they go to it, back'n'forth. Finally he says, "Matilda! Ya said ya'd do it!" An she stands up an she says, "I will do it!"

So I get down with my back to a big rock. An I tell her, climb up on the rock. Put one foot one side a my neck, one foot t'other side. "No!" she says. She aint gonna do that. She's gonna put both legs ta one side. Ride me sidesaddle!

Wal, that would a tipped us over fer sure. I wouldn't a heered the end of it. Cause that water wahnt more'n two shakes more'n a cake a ice. An she knew it. But she says, "No!" Tween you'n'me, I doubt that woman ever had her legs round any man's neck.

Dolly's gigglin, cause she's goin next. Finally Mr. Fieldin says, "Listen ta me, Matilda. Put yer delicacy"—No. He says "Put yer"—Oh. He says "ferget." He says, "Ferget yer delicacy and do what Mr. Nye says." She looked kind a surprised when he said that.

So she puts one leg over an packs in her petty-coats—like she's packin me ta go ta Saratogy. An she puts t'other leg over. An she sets down real easy. But when I move away from the rock, she slides down my back.

Wal, I tell her that won't do. She's gotta hitch-up so's I can walk. So she grabs hole a my hair. An packs in her petty-coats.

I lay my hans on her feet ta steady em. Cause they're kickin all over. But my hans on her feet tickles her, an she gets ta wigglin an jigglin an pullin on them petty-coats. I tell ya, I never knew a woman had that many movin parts. Haulin that woman was like haulin a sack a coons.

Soon's I get'n the water she's slidin down again. I try ta get under an flip her up. But she's got so damn low our heads're even.

Dolly an Mr. Fieldin see what's goin on. He yells at her, "Hitch-up, Matilda!"

So she throws her arm round my neck. An all I can see is skyrockets.

We're gettin near deep water. Dolly's yellin, "Ride yer horsie, Auntie!" An she's slippin down again. I'm thinkin I'm gonna have ta switch ends ta keep her up. But then I think soon she feels that water on her behind, she'll hitch-up.

Sure nuf. I get one foot in deep water an UP! she hitches. Straight as a general. Digs in her heels like she's got wolves on her trail. "That's it!" Mr. Fieldin yells. "Hitch-up, Matilda!" An leanin way over I got her through.

An then . . . wal—

No. That's all I'm tellin.

Several kinds of walkway have been built to span the water at the walled end of Avalanche Lake. Some have floated on logs. Others, including the present span, have rested on supports embedded in the rock. But whatever form these walkways take, they are always called the "hitch-up matilda."

THE LAST TARRIN'N'FEATHERIN

Location: Warren County?, 1870s?

Source: Jeanne Robert Foster, *Adirondack Portraits* (1986). Copyright © 1986 by Noel Riedinger-Johnson. Retold by permission of Syracuse University Press.

Foster grew up in Warren, Essex, and Hamilton Counties during the 1880s and 90s.

Also from Foster: "The Lumberjack's Tale," 49; "Nance's Baby," 35; "The Old Church," 133; "Sonny's Coat," 71

We had our own ways a doin things back then. When it come ta law'n'order, we follered Deacon Bowes. He said the best thing was ride law breakers out a town after they was tarred'n'feathered. He kept the tar ready, an we all saved our chicken feathers.

So they spoke ta Deacon Bowes bout Sal Pheemy an that man come ta live with her. They was livin out a wedlock, an that man was a lot younger'n Sal. Folks was worried a long time bout goins-on at that Hoadley place. An they wanted a tarrin'n' featherin.

The Deacon said he'd go home'n'pray'n'read the Lord's word. Now that's the kind a man ya look up to. He was in his pew every Sunday, faithful, always givin good advice ta the young folks. An he was a fine figger of a man, too—tall with longish hair combed back. An a Roman nose. Strangers when they seen him, they said he looked jest like George Washington.

So they spoke ta the Deacon, an after a time he said we'd have the tarrin'n' featherin. But he kept puttin it off. Week goin on month. Till he was took sick. An finally he was laid away. An still nuthin was done bout old Sal.

She was gone away a long time. Years back it was. Nobody knew where. Then she come home. All her folks was gone. An now a man lived there.

They never come ta church er went neighborin. Folks seen him helpin her out'n the field. An sometimes they seen him at night when the lamp was lit. They seen him inside there. An folks that tried ta live decent'n'godly, they wanted a tarrin'n' featherin.

So one day we picked up Sal an the man an fetched em down in a lumber wagon. The Deacon had a place in Cedar Holler. His kettle was settin there with the tar in it. An we all brought our chicken feathers.

When we untied em, Sal stood up'n'said, "Don't touch the boy. I'm the sinner."

An the man stepped in front a her an said, "Don't hurt my ma. She aint well. I wouldn't a come home only I was sick."

"His ma?" The boys laughed at him. "Sal never married. He's lyin! Who's his pa?"

The man tore off his cap. We looked at his forehead, the Roman nose, the mouth. It was a younger Deacon Bowes.

We remembered how the Deacon was always puttin off the tarrin'n'featherin. An we thought a Sal goin away years back, never comin home er sendin word. An the thought come how mebby every man sometime comes ta judgment.

We took em home an left em on the doorstep.

That was our last tarrin'n'featherin.

THE HUNTER'S TALE

Location: told at Little Ampersand Pond, Franklin County, 1856
Source: "Fides," "A Marvellous Hunting Story," *The Spirit of the Times* (27 September 1856)
This is the earliest-known tall tale in the Adirondacks. The guide who told it is unknown, as is the city sport who heard it and signed himself "Fides."

One time—It was when Dr. Cutler come up. Him an his dad used ta camp on them rocks there over the marsh. They wahnt ones fer walkin. They liked their huntin ground all laid out front of em.

Wal, this time Cutler come up early, by hisself. He wanted ta play a trick. He wanted us ta get a bear an play a trick on his dad.

That's a waste of a bear I says—ta myself. I told his dad we'd get one. Let him wait till his dad come. So on our way ta find the bear, I found us some tracks. Get his mind on somethin else.

An somethin did go by. I wahnt sure what. Somethin like a deer. It was headed fer our salt lick. Old Heck, he got a good smell. Lot a dew on the grass.

You 'member old Heck? Ay-uh. He was fore yer time.

Wal, I never had a better huntin dog. He wahnt fast like Range there. But old Heck never lied. When he yelled, ya knew somethin was up. Somethin was up an headed fer water. Old Heck never lied.

Then he went an ketched his foot in one a Harve's bear traps. Four days after I found him. Thin as a holla worm. An he wahnt much good after that.

An that's one bear trap's done ketchin dogs. Last I knowed it was still huntin bull-heads. Yep. Down the bottom a Mud Pond.

Anyways, there we was, me an old Heck. Cutler said he'd hang back an take care a some business.

Wal, we wahnt hardly ta the foot a Burnt Hill an Heck begun ta snuff. He lays down, shiverin. Shiverin all over. So I loosed him.

He give a bound. An a yell. He cut through a thicket a birch. He run in there. Cracklin. An out comes a . . . wal, a specimen. A specimen.

I thought I seen everythin. But this here was a specimen.

It was somethin like a deer. But that wahnt no deer tail. That was a wolf tail. Big bushy tail, bout three foot long. No horns. Color—oh, somethin like a mully cow.

Wal, off they run. So I head over the hill fer the runway. But I wahnt but half up the hill, an here comes Heck, runnin roun the bottom. Drivin that varmint roun again!

So I run down, tried ta cut em off. Sure wahnt like any chasin I ever seen. But fore I got to em, they was gone roun up ahead.

The track was like a deer. But the claws was wider. The dew claws was wider. An they made big holes. An the holes on the downhill side was deeper.

Wal, I headed back up the hill. The runnin nearly done me in!

Then I says ta myself, mebby that critter aint headed fer water. Mebby he's trying another tack. So I found a clear place, down long the bottom, where they used ta burn coal. I set down. Leaned the rifle. Took out a plug a tobacca.

Sure nuf. Heck was makin good time. I heered him on the left. The bushes crackled. I grabbed the gun. An when the smoke clears, Heck has him by the haunches. He's dead as a smelt.

Now right here's the real story.

That critter, he was lyin belly up. An his legs straight up in the air. An if that aint somethin, two a them legs on one side was bout half a length shorter than the two legs on t'other side! Yep. That critter had two short legs on one side and two long legs on t'other.

I fired a couple shots fer Cutler. An I set down on a log.

Yep. This here was a specimen all right. That sideshow fella—that Barnum—Barnum, he'd pay a price fer this.

Then Cutler comes up. He takes one look at him, an he says, "By jove! I thought they was all kilt off."

"Kilt off?" I says. "All what kilt off?"

So Cutler rolls him over. He looks at them short legs. He shakes his head. "I never thought I'd live ta see one," he says.

"See what?" I says. Them city folks. Think they know everythin.

He rolls him back an looks at the long legs on the downhill side. "Jared," he says, "this here's a haggletopelter."

"A haggletopelter?"

"Ya must a heered a em," he says.

"I ben huntin these woods twenty-three years," I says. "An I aint never heered a sech a thing."

So what's he do? He tells me how his dad got one. Over on Round Hill. Looked jist like mine. The critter jumped out of a thicket. His dad was pickin berries. The critter jumps out of a thicket. So his dad takes after him.

Now, thing is, what they do is they run roun side hills. That's what the legs're built for. An after his dad chased him roun the hill three, four time, he calated he'd turn roun, head him off.

So he turns roun. Starts backtrackin. Wal, the critter hoves up an sees him. An his dad says the critter must a forgot hisself. Cause he jumped roun. An that put his long legs on the uphill side. An he topples over. Belly up. Jist like mine.

I'll tell ya what I was gonna do. I was gonna show him off. But we had ta git some trout. An when we come back from Raquette Falls—Damndest luck!

I had him skinned out, hung on a pole. Wal, wolves must a smelt him, cause we found a trail where wolves drug him off. That's why ya don't see many of em. Cause wolves git em.

Cutlers? Wal, he said he didn't know what happened ta the one his dad got. He was too young then.

Yep. Them haggletopelters, they aint smart, but they still git away from ya.

The "haggletopelter" appears in hills folklore from Maine to Texas. It is usually called a "sidehill gouger." This Adirondack version predates all other published accounts by more than fifty years. See Richard M. Dorson, *Man and Beast in American Comic Legend* (1982), 29-35. The haggletopelter also appears in "The Animules," 117, where it has horns and lacks the wolf tail.

THE CAPTAIN'S TALE

Location: the shore of Lake Champlain, Essex County, 1850s?
Source: Philander Deming, *Adirondack Stories* (1880)
Also from Deming: "The Huckleberry Pickers," 31; "Little Willie," 45

A tall, muscular woman stands at the door of her log house high above the Champlain Valley. She squints toward a bay some ten miles off. Specks are discernible on the trembling water and by long, long watching, the specks can be seen moving slowly to and fro.

One of the specks nears the bay and at length enters it. The woman goes indoors for a spyglass. The lens is cracked. All it gives is a smokey view. But that's enough. A certain angle in the rigging tells her the *Dolly Ann* is back.

Jupiter looked up when she went inside. Now he gets up and stretches himself. He approaches her with a wriggling in his hind quarters. He has his own way of knowing. He looks toward the road, then back at the woman. He shakes himself and gives her a long steady gaze. She nods. That's all it takes. He's off and over the fence and down the road. The woman goes back indoors.

About four o'clock a husky young man came swinging up the road with the dog. "Heigh-ho, mother!"

"How do you do, John?"

That's all they said, but there was more that passed between them. For the man had a bright look on his face, and there was a tremor in the woman's voice.

Two hours pass. After supper some neighbors come up to visit. They'd seen John with the dog. "Where's yer cousin William?"

He didn't answer directly. He seemed uneasy. Finally he said he'd quarreled with William. They had words and blows. William jumped ship and went off somewhere. Canada he supposed. He didn't know where, and he didn't care.

A month goes by. It's August.

Stories begin coming up the lake from Canada. At the mouth of Fish River, just over the line, a swollen, festering corpse had risen and floated among the ships. Two boatmen fished it out and buried it. They said it was the body of a young man. He was about the height, size, and appearance of cousin William.

And another story, this one told by the captain of a sloop moored near John's ship at the mouth of Fish River. He said he heard quarreling. All afternoon it went on. He thought they were drinking. There was a lull at nightfall. Then it broke out again. The captain saw nothing—it was too dark—but he heard angry words. Then blows, a thud, a plunge in the water.

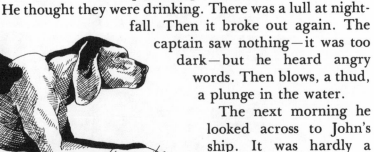

The next morning he looked across to John's ship. It was hardly a stone's throw from his own. He saw a hat lying on the deck. Looking through his spyglass, he saw spatters of blood. He didn't think it any of his business, and when a breeze came up, he sailed away. But then he heard about the floating corpse.

And so, rather quickly, it came to be the opinion up and down the lake that Captain John had killed his cousin. Neighbors on the Essex road said the same thing. He ought to be arrested.

Accordingly, on a raw day in November, two officers climbed up the road and arrested him. There was a trembling about the mother's mouth as she spoke to them. John looked pale. Yet quietly, without complaint, he made ready. "Don't worry, mother. It will all be made right."

"Yes, John. I know."

The men take John down the road to the next house where they left their team. Jupiter watches, his front paws up on the fence. Gradually his tail stops wagging, and when the men pass round the turn, he drops down and goes back to the house.

A sharp wind tore through the mountains that night, a freezing wind from the north. The trees snapped and howled.

At midnight the woman and dog leave the house. She fastens the door. They start down the road. The next day, at noon, very weary, they put up at a hotel near the county jail.

The trial lasted three days. The captain of the sloop told his story. The two boatmen who'd found the body told theirs. The men who'd been the crew of John's ship were called, but they were on shore when it happened. All they knew was that when they got back, William was gone.

The judge thought the evidence against John was convincing. But the counsel John's mother employed took the ground that the crime was committed in Canada. The courts in New York had no jurisdiction. This view prevailed, and John was released.

But the story was not over. It was passed from mouth to mouth. It traveled far into Canada and down to Washington. A murderer was living on the shore of Lake Champlain. It was only the tricks of a lawyer that got him off.

In time formal application was made for the delivery into Canada of one John Wilson, believed guilty of the murder of his cousin. And once again two officers climbed up the road. They were fighting a snowstorm this time. A neighbor had to guide them. But in half an hour they were back outside with their prisoner.

The next four months were long and hard for the mother. Morning, noon, and night she had to be out in the cold, tending the cow, the sheep, cutting wood, dragging it through the snow, chopping it up. A few neighbors tried to help. But the nearest lived a mile away. And, as they all agreed, she was the mother of a murderer.

She got two letters from John. The first said he was imprisoned and awaiting trial. The second said his trial was set for early March. That was all she heard. The lake froze and the mailboats stopped running.

When March came and went without word, it was generally assumed he'd been convicted. When the mailboats came again, the neighbors looked for a letter or newspaper announcing his execution.

On a windy day in April, with birds twittering about the clearing, the mother climbs up on a ridge back of the house. She turns toward the lake. She can see . . . three, four boats.

She doesn't notice the man who comes up the road and through the gate. When he rounds the house, a spasm crosses her face. "John!" She climbs down. As she approaches him she seems to struggle with herself. He doesn't lift his eyes.

They go indoors. The woman begins to spread the table. John goes out back to cut wood. Afterwards he sits by the stove. It's the way they always did it.

But this time there was a great sadness. Jupiter could feel it. He didn't frisk. He seemed tired. He merely came up and lay with his head on John's boot.

At supper John talked about his food in jail and about his life there. "Do you go back?"

"No. It is finished." The judge had not found enough evidence to convict him.

John's ship lay idle that spring. He said he needed to rest. But the truth was he saw a great change in his mother. Her resources were exhausted. Her spirit was gone. The change was not yet apparent to others, but it was to him.

When the dandelions began to bloom, she stopped moving about much. She sat by the open door. She sat there the most of every day, gazing. And she wept. She no longer tried to hold her feelings. She wept, and she told John of her early loves, the good times of her girlhood. He learned more of his mother's heart, there on the doorstep, than he had learned in all the years before. She was counting over with him the treasures of her life.

There was no great scene when she died. It happened quietly, at evening, as July was coming on. She had wept much in the morning. As the day grew warm she became faint. At noon John moved her back to her bed. And there she died as the sun went down.

John spent that night alone with her. Since his return only one neighbor was willing to call, and he lived two miles away. John did not want to trouble him.

He lighted a candle. He took down the Bible and hymnal—the ones his mother had carried twice a week to the schoolhouse that served as church. And there, alone with the dead, he spent the hours of dark in reading and remembrance.

At dawn John locked the door and went over to Pete's. Then he went down to the village to tell Downer and get the things. Downer was the minister, and "the things" were a coffin and a shroud.

The funeral was held on Thursday. Pete took care to have the neighbors there, though it hardly seemed John wanted them. He stood apart. They still held him guilty. It was only the tricks of a lawyer that got him off.

John chose to bury his mother not in the village burying ground but at home on their own land. And so, in a little hollow, just under the ridge, he laid his mother to rest.

Eleven years go by.

John gained respect but not friendship. His lawyer advised him to leave the lake, but John chose to stay. And after every trip he spent a day or two at the old place.

He built a picket fence around his mother's grave. The neighbors talked about the headstone he carried up on a wagon. Pete saw him one night standing out on the ridge. Even in winter, when he boarded down by the lake, he made many trips up to the homestead.

Eleven years . . .

It's June. John stands in the doorway, looking out toward the lake and beyond to the mountains.

Three men come round the bend. They see him. They come up the road. They turn in at the gate. They come up to where he stands. One of them steps forward and looks John in the eye. "John, don't you know me?"

"William?"

The other two step forward. They were once John's warmest friends. They take his arm. They tell him of William's return. They beg his forgiveness.

They want him to come home with them. All his old friends will be there. But John isn't sure. They press. But he seems to be dreaming. He asks over and over, "William? Is it you?" He looks round and falls.

The men carry him indoors. They hadn't expected this. They fan him with their hats. They splash water on his face.

For two months John lay in bed. The neighbors came and took care of him. But many days it seemed their kindness pained him. "It looks like as if a mean word don't hurt him none. But a kind one he can't take."

As he recovered, his manner grew more and more shrinking. Yet it won him a strange affection. In later years it was said he became the best loved man on the lake. He never had trouble with his crews. Children clung to his hands when he came ashore. And the woman who married him, it is said, died of grief when he passed away.

Even now John sleeps among us, with his wife and mother beside him, in a grassy hollow, just under a ridge, where an old wilderness road used to wind its way into the mountains.

THE LEGEND OF SACANDAGA LAKE

for Kent Busman

Location: Sacandaga Lake, Hamilton County, time of the Mohawks
Source: Charles Fenno Hoffman, *Wild Scenes in the Forest and Prairie* (1839)
This is the earliest-known guide's story in the Adirondacks. It was told to Hoffman (1806-1884), a writer from New York City, in 1837. The guide is unknown. The language style and some local details in this version are derived from the journals of Oliver W. Whitman, a guide from Wells, as transcribed in Donald R. Williams, *Oliver H. Whitman, Adirondack Guide* (1979)

See them rocks? Big ones? Ones climbin out the water? Them's Injun rocks. Ya see em all over. Been here since before thunder. No man knows what Injuns they was.

They used ta come summertime. Camp out. Go huntin. Like city folks. Didn't live here. No. It's us got stuff ta grow. Wahnt no watermelons an plum trees when Injuns was here.

Oh, some of em's okay.

Not them rock Injuns, though. They was mean.

Ya see em out the woods. Hidin. Waitin for ya.

There's one of em bigger'n the rest. Nuthin grows there. I an Allen put a line a traps back there. Didn't ketch a cussed thing. Cause a that Injun rock.

If ya look close, ya can see how it's a big head. Ya can see the nose. Where the eyes was. There's ferns up top. The jaw's fell down so there's a big crack. Ferns comin outta there.

Tom Clemons says it used ta—He's game proctor, Tom Clemons. He says used ta be bigger. I don know where he gets that notion. It's close on sixty-five foot. But Tom Clemons says used ta be big as the whole clearin. An that's why nuthin grows there.

Yeah, them rock Injuns was mean. Always fightin. They had this lake, lots a others. But then they had bad times.

It aint always good like now. Two year 'go we had a storm tore the big hill all ta

pieces. An a big fire up Finch Moun'n. An the cold—Wal, I seen snow end a July, corn snow. It gets so dry this crick here don have spit ta lick.

Dr. Fairwell says this used ta be ice—all this, all over. He says the ice was a mile high. I don know as I believe it. I guided Dr. Fairwell. He can't hardly tie his shoe.

He can't hardly tie his shoe less'n there's someone there ta hold it for him. But if there be ice a mile high, it don be worse'n when there's no snow Jan-wary an no rain July.

So one a them rock Injuns gets the notion ta clear out. Nother says no, they can't. They got enemies all round. Nother says no, they'll lose their lakes. Never get em back. So the first says, "Okay, let's clear out fer good. This place aint doin us no good."

Then the elders speaks up. "What'll we et?" That's what the elders wants ta know. "What'll we et?" An besides, there's ancestors. Can't run off, leave them.

Now Injuns, they say dead folks can help ya or hurt ya. Depends on how ya treat em. I don know how I think bout that. Looks ta me when yer dead yer gone. But . . . I hear them Injun rocks.

Some nights end a June ya wake up an ya hear cryin. Cryin here. Cryin there. Aint loons. Aint cats. Aint wolves.

An ya see somethin white blowin on the water. Only it's got legs in it. Hunderds a legs.

An ya hear flappin. Like wings. Only it's got wings from here ta All-Benny. Then somethin shoves the white stuff over by them rocks.

Next thing, dead quiet.

Ya know when ya put yer head down a ice cave? Cold air hits yer face? That's how it feels. Feels jes like that.

Wal, them elders, they say they can't go cause the Great Spirit's puttin a test to em. No matter where they go, Spirit's gonna find em. They gotta make up fer what they done wrong.

An that gets the young-uns crabid. "What wrong they taking bout? We aint done wrong. Must be the old folks done it. We aint done wrong."

One of em gets ta jumpin, yellin. Bout how the old folks is tryin ta kill em, starve em. An he gets em all, all of em worked up.

Then they done a terrible thing. They done what no man oughta do. No man. Injun er white.

They turned on them old folks. Took their tomahawks an split their heads open. Like they was choppin stove wood. The women folks run ever which way. An the kids with em. Who knows? Maybe they's next.

Wal, after a terrible thing like that they oughta gone an cleared out. Never come back. But somethin held em.

First, they was gonna put the old folks ta rest. No tellin what bad come if they didn't do it. So they made a big fire an burned em. Only first they cut off the heads. An the heads, they put em in Sacandaga Lake.

Where they get a notion like that? But they thought the Spirit was gonna like it.

So they done it.

Built a huge big fire up on the ridge. Must a cut down a acre a trees. Nuthin ever grew there again. Black smoke the whole day.

Then they took the heads an put each of em in a canoe. Seven of em. Took em out on the lake. Long line of em.

The Injun what started it, he took each head. One by one. Tied it ta the rest. By the hair. An he tied a big rock to em.

But when he got holt a the last head, his canoe split down the middle. Like a clap a thunder. He jumped. But he got caught. In the heads. In the hair. Pulled him under. He was screamin. An blood was gushin up.

Other Injuns, they hightailed fer shore. When they looked round, blood was boilin up.

Wal, there again they oughta cleared out. But they didn't. It don make no sense. But somethin held em.

Next morning they seed the lake was wrong. When a wind blowed, nuthin moved. Nuthin. Like it was froze. Next day, same thing.

But third day it begun ta move. Somethin was comin up. Crick slime er somethin? No. It was somethin black.

Them braves was scared most to a fit. But they didn't move. Somethin was makin em watch.

Fourth day somethin else come up. Under the black. Somethin solid. Under the water. An the black was floatin out. Like clumps a hair.

Fifth day, forenoon, they seen what it was. A head. A big head. They was hidin in the trees, wonderin what ta do. Afternoon it rizzed up like a rock island. Black hair floatin off.

Sixth day a forehead was showin. An the tips a two big ears. Seventh day, two big eyes. One a them squaws come along. When she seed them eyes lookin at her, an blinkin, she took off. An that's the last they seen a their squaws.

Eighth day an ninth it rizzed out an floated. An it kept growin. Black hair runnin down. Round the eyes. An the eyes lookin round.

Then somethin else come up. Under it. A wind come along. It was wings. Big wings. With claws on the end.

Nother wind come. The wings spread out cross the lake. The head rizzed up, up, over the trees. Made a shadow 'cross that whole lake.

Some a them Injuns was scared to a fit. Somethin bout them eyes watchin em. An them claws. They's ones got left behind. Probly they's ones in them rocks there.

Other Injuns, they run. All night they run. Quiet, way Injuns run.

Then one of em hears somethin. It's wings! They get down a cave. But the ground shook under em. An the eyes burned through, give em nightmares. Next night they run again.

No matter. That head kept after em.

Some of em was climbin a mountain west a here. They get ta the head of a crick. Big eyes watchin em! Big wings beatin the ground! They run this way, that way.

No matter. That head kept after em. Ever one. One by one.

Didn't touch em, though. Not one. It teased em. Like a barn cat'n'a bird. Wore em down. Real slow. An nex mornin they's a big rock where the Injun was.

Ya see em up the sides a mountains. Hangin on. Like nex minute they's gonna fall. Ya see em bent over, middle of a crick. Ya can always tell em. Ya see em under a tree, roots tyin em down.

There was a city man wrote bout em in the All-Benny paper. "It hath tell-tale tongues, this easin air that wails an cries. Where come these wandrin sighs? What gory deed—" He wrote it like that.

Don sound ta me like that man knows. When ya hear cryin end a June—cryin here, cryin there. That cryin, that aint no "easin air." You tell me what that cryin is if it aint them Injun rocks.

THE LAKE GEORGE EPITAPH

Source: *The Lake George Mirror*, 1881
My thanks to Jean Hadden who discovered this epitaph in an old scrapbook and published it in her local history column in *The Adirondack Journal* (Warrensburg).

Here lies a poor woman who always was tired,
Who lived in a house where help was not hired.
Her last days on earth she said, "Friends, I'm a-goin
Where washin aint done, nor cookin nor sewin,
Where everthing's jest ta all a my wishes.
(An cause they don't eat, there's no doin dishes.)
Don't weep fer me now. Don't weep fer me never.
Cause I'm doin nuthin fer ever an ever!"

A-HUNTING OF THE DEER

Location: Keene Valley, Essex County, 1870s
Source: Charles Dudley Warner, *In the Wilderness* (1876)
Also from Warner: "How I Got a Bear," 123; "Old Mountain Phelps," 65

It's early morning on Basin Mountain. A doe is feeding. The night was warm and showery, and so far the day has opened in an undecided way. The wind is southerly now — what the deer call a dog wind. They know the meaning of a southerly wind and a cloudy sky.

The sole companion of the doe is a little fawn, her first born. His coat is mottled with spots. They make him lovely as a gazelle.

His father is far away. He spent the night over at Clear Pond, ostensibly to eat lilies, but the pond is also a fashionable retreat among the deer. Perhaps the doe remembers him there last summer.

Her fawn has had his morning milk and lies curled up on a bed of moss. With large brown eyes he watches his mother. From time to time as she crops the leaves of young shoots, she turns to look at him. If she steps too far away, he makes a movement as if to rise. But he's quickly reassured when she turns her gaze on him. If he bleats, she bounds to him at once and licks his skin until it shines.

The doe herself is a beauty. She has slender limbs, a round body, an aristocratic head with tall ears and luminous eyes. Look at the pose she makes when she lifts her head and looks back at her fawn.

Then she looks to the south. She examines the air.

Perhaps it was only the wind she heard. The woods are always full of moans and premonitions. If her suspicions are excited for an instant, they're gone just as soon, and with a glance back at her infant, she continues to pick up her breakfast.

But wait! There was a sound!

She turned to the south. The cry was repeated. A tremor ran through her limbs. It was a long sliding note, the baying of a hound.

It was still far off, though — at the foot of the mountain. She bounded away. But her fawn started up with a bleat, and she returned. She bent over and licked his face. "Come," she seemed to say, "follow me."

The little one struggled up and stumbled after her. She bounded ahead and waited. He tumbled over a log.

He was groggy and whined. He didn't hear the hound, and perhaps if the dog had rushed him, he would have tried to make friends with it.

She nudged and urged him on by all the means at her command. But it was slow going for his wobbly legs. Alone she might have been a mile away by now. Together they'd made only a few rods. Whenever he caught up, he wanted to play.

He wanted more milk. But his mother wouldn't stand still. She moved on continually, and his little legs got caught in the roots of the path.

Then came a sound that threw her into a panic—a sharp yelp and a prolonged babble of howls. One of the dogs had caught her scent. The pack was closing in. She couldn't crawl on like this. She turned again for flight. But her little one tumbled over and bleated.

Once more she returned, her head erect, her nostrils distended. She was quivering like a mimosa.

Her fawn began to nurse. The baying grew nearer, but she let him finish. He took all he wanted and lay down again. She bent down and licked his face. Then, with the swiftness of a bird, she shot through the forest.

By any human standard she was heading toward the jaws of death. Her course was straight toward the hounds. But human calculations are often selfish.

She leaped down the mountain till she reached a forest of hardwood. The cries of the pack echoed distinctly in the open spaces. Judging they were not far off, she turned north. Presently she heard a yelp of discovery and the howls of pursuit. The dogs had struck her trail. Her fawn was safe.

On she bounded at a slapping pace. For the moment fear left her and she felt the exhilaration of the chase. She cleared the moose bushes, flying over fallen logs, pausing neither for brook nor ravine. The baying of the hounds grew fainter.

But then she struck a deadwood slash. It was marvelous to see her leaping through its intricacies. No other animal could have done it. But it was killing work. She began to pant, and she lost ground. The baying grew nearer. Slowly she worked her way up a slope till once more on level ground she stretched away.

After running another half mile at top speed, she turned west, intending by a wide circuit to return to her fawn. But just then she heard another hound. It was in the very direction she wanted to go! She swerved again. There was nothing to do but keep to the north.

In five minutes more she reached a clearing. The smell of cows washed over her. On down the hill with other clearings broken by fences and patches of woods. And a mile or two farther lay a valley and the shining Ausable River.

Somewhere down there a door slammed. She stopped short. Voices drifted up. Windows were gleaming. But there was no choice. The noise of the pack was close behind her. She must cross that valley and gain the mountain opposite.

She leaped ahead—and stopped again. A dog was barking on her right. In a panic she turned left and flew down the mountain toward the houses.

It was a thrilling sight to see her clear the fences, but what a shot she was. Perhaps someone would have spared her life and shut her up in a barn and fed her. But was there anyone in all that valley who would let her go back to her fawn?

She turned by the saw mill and gained a woodpath, just as the hounds came tumbling over the hill. With a burst of speed she cleared the stream. A bullet cut the air ahead of her. Sulphur stung her nose. She leaped into the road beside a wagonload of hay. A man and a boy with pitchforks came running.

There was clambering and shouting as she fled toward town. Women and children ran to see her. The men snatched their rifles. At the boarding houses people came out and cheered.

Shots were fired.

A camp stool was thrown from the veranda.

Some boys shooting in the meadow popped away at her, but they were used to a target that stood still, and they missed.

Twenty more people were about to fire when she leaped a fence and sped toward the foothills.

For days after, her flight was talked about, and the summer boarders kept their guns handy, expecting other deer would follow along to be shot at.

The doe went slower now, evidently fatigued if not frightened half to death. Nothing is more appalling to a recluse than a houseful of summer boarders.

As she gained the woods a rabble of people started across the meadow. Then the dogs, panting and lolling out their tongues. When she was back in the timber, she heard their yelps spreading out across the field.

Her courage was not gone. She was game to the tips of her ears. But the pace she'd been keeping told on her. Her legs trembled and her heart beat like a trip hammer.

She slowed her speed, keeping to the right of a stream. When she'd gone a couple of miles and the dogs were gaining again, she crossed the brook and climbed a steep bank. This fording of the stream threw the hounds off for a while. The doe pushed on till their uncertain barks were faint in her ears. Then she dropped to the ground.

Brief as it was, this rest saved her life. Roused again by the baying pack, she jumped forward. It was still a race with death, but the odds were better.

Going now slower, now faster, as the pursuit seemed distant or near, she worked her way through a maze of swamps and ravines under Haystack Mountain. Some instinct still kept her away from her fawn. At intervals she lay down, her limbs

unsteady. Then spurred on by the cry of the dogs she leaped ahead. Finally she raced down a shoulder of Barlett Mountain towards a lake.

At her first step in the water she sprang back. A boat was on the lake. Two men were in it. One was rowing. The other held a gun.

She looked behind her. The dogs were coming down the hill.

She plunged into the lake as the boat rushed towards her. She turned. The boat turned.

There was a splash and a gun roar. "Confound it!" The rattle of oars. The sting of sulphur.

She turned back towards shore. But the dogs were already there, lapping at the water. She turned again, her eyes wild with fear.

With a rush of water the boat was upon her. The man at the oars leaned over and grabbed her tail. "Knock her over the head with the paddle." The other man took a paddle and swung it overhead. But just then the doe looked up at him.

"Jim . . . No, I can't do it. Let her go."

"Let thunder go!"

The man at the oars slung her round by the tail, whipped out his hunting knife, and slit her throat. That night the sport and his guide ate venison.

In the early afternoon, as the doe was making her way through those marshes by Haystack Mountain, the buck returned. The fawn had been bleating for hours. The buck sniffed the fear of his doe, still hovering in the brush. The fawn nuzzled him and appealed for milk. But the buck had nothing to give him. He listened in one direction . . . then the other. Then he turned away with a nervous kick of his leg. The little one stumbled after him.

In the years following publication of this story, four elements in it were outlawed in New York and elsewhere: hunting does, hunting with dogs, hunting in summer, and killing deer in water.

MOTHER

Location: Lewis, Essex County, 1880s

Source: Edna West Teall, *Adirondack Tales* (1970). Copyright ©
1970 by Adirondack Life magazine. Retold by permission.

Mrs. Teall (1881-1968) was born and raised on a farm in the
Champlain Valley. Later, for thirty years, she was Women's Page
Editor of the *Newark Evening News* in New Jersey.

What I remember most is her face at the window. The smell of clover always brings it to mind.

First thing every morning she looked out to see if the day would be stormy or clear. Then she glanced at the road to see if anyone was passing by. It might be a neighbor on an early trip to the village, or the men off to work. She knew them all and their interests. If a stranger went by, this was a real item of news. Who was it? Where was he going? Those minutes by the window were her morning newspaper.

Then all through the day she looked out to see what the men were doing. Should she have dinner ready when they brought this load of hay? Or would they want to draw one more? She kept a pencil and slip of paper hanging by the window, and whenever the haywagon pulled up she marked down a line. To her those wagonloads were interest on the mortgage or new clothes for winter, and the men brought their loads up the road like offerings to a shrine.

If a team passed outside, mother ran to see if company was coming. We had no close neighbors, and the mail came only once or twice a week. So visitors supplied most of the news and gossip.

A wagon rattling down the west hill might be grampa. A team on the north hill could be anyone. "Edna! Come look!" It was gypsies. "Where do you suppose they're going?"

Or it might be the packpeddler. He was a walking five-and-dime with yard goods, rings, buttons, needles— all carried in two big packs. Sometimes he stayed overnight. He'd tell us all the goings-on up and down the lake. If he stayed, mother charged him fifty cents, but next morning when he opened his packs, she always found more than fifty cents worth of goods to buy from him.

Our house stood high above the road, nestled in lilacs. It looked bigger than it really was, and its brick Georgian face seemed to peer down rather regally at the sandy tracks outside. "It's so cool in summer," the neighbors would say, "and so warm in winter"—which was true. No wind or blizzard could penetrate those walls. And the bricks never looked frowzy the way wooden houses did when they needed paint.

Sometimes we heard a train whistle off in the distance. It was usually at twilight. For miles we could follow it in and out of the coves along the lakeshore. We pictured it glowing with light, the people relaxing in big velvet chairs or dining at tables with snow-white linen, silver, brown-skinned waiters. We always wondered about people who could travel so luxuriously. We imagined they must all be very rich with big houses to live in.

A whippoorwill might settle on our parlor steps. He was always so intent. Sometimes his mate joined him and they made a lot of gurgling sounds together. The cows in the barn stomped and moo-ed. Across the meadow a coon might scream. Or the silence was broken by the distant hoot of an owl.

Indoor work took most of mother's time. She had three big meals to cook every day, the house to clean. Every morning she washed and polished the oil lamps. She made father's shirts, her own dresses and mine, all our underwear, even the petticoats.

There was a party dress of hers I remember. It was made of black cashmere with bands of moire silk. There were small panels at the sides and long flat revers down the front with black and gold buttons. When she wore it, instead of tying her hair back in a knot, her sister or one of the younger women would comb it high up in a French twist. She could look so elegant.

She knitted our socks, made rugs and quilts. Every day she skimmed the milk, and twice a week she made butter. In spring she made lye soap, and in summer there were trips outdoors for vegetables and berries.

There was sweet corn to cook and dry for winter, tomatoes to can, pumpkins and apples to dry, preserves and jellies and pickles to make. In the fall father helped her make sausage and preserve the meat. But no matter how long it took, mother tried out the lard herself.

If she were alive today, she'd probably take an active part in outdoor work as well. But mother was trained in a different school. She could cook and sew or grieve and pray, but a lady did not go into the hayfield. It was a strict code inherited from her mother and grandmother. It had marked the neighborhood for generations. Father couldn't help teasing her about it. One time when we had company from town, he called out, "Mary, have you fed the pigs yet?" I don't think she ever forgave him for that.

On washdays in freezing weather he'd hang the clothes for her while she coached from the window. But he always left a twist of his own. "Land sakes, Edna! He hangs em so crooked." There they were, the longjohns with their arms and legs frozen at all angles, the sheets up on one side and down the other. "What'll the neighbors think, Edna?"

One day she and I went to the village with a tub of her butter and a list of things she needed. It was an unwritten law that butter and egg money belonged to the wife. There were two stores. The owner of one was known for his surliness, but he had the better line of goods, so mother stopped there.

He went out to the buggy and brought in the tub. But it was one of his bad days. He reached behind the counter for a long, thin rod. It was a tester. You twisted it down through the butter, and when you pulled it out, you could see if the bottom layers were stale.

Mother was furious. No storekeeper had ever tested her butter before. "Please put the cover on and take the tub back to the buggy." She turned and walked out. "The very idea! Never in all my life! Edna, we're going to Mr. Henry's store."

There she was treated properly. "Ah, Mrs. West . . . Yes, yes. I'll bring it right in." Mr. Henry carried it right down cellar. But mother was still sputtering on the way home.

One thing that took a good deal of her time was neighboring. She was a good neighbor not only because she liked it but because it was needed. Nowadays you're called a neighbor simply because you live nearby. But in mother's time a neighbor was someone you could count on. When you were sick, it was a neighbor who came to watch so your own family could get a few hours rest. When death came, it was a neighbor who prepared the body for burial.

It often happened that mother was called on. And it mattered not if it was high noon or three o'clock in the morning. Someone might have a broken arm or a baby on the way. Help was needed.

There were long drives over rough country roads drifted with snow or gullied by rain. The darkness bore down as though to hold you back. But how welcome you were. Now the family could creep away to bed. But first they set out a midnight lunch for you and covered it with an extra cloth.

How the wind moaned those lonely nights. How the rain dashed against the windows. Two o'clock. A whole hour had passed and still no doctor. The very silence seemed to carry you out on an ocean of uncertainty. Three, four. A faint glimmer in the east. Five, six. At last the voices of day.

House plants were mother's favorite hobby. Winter mornings she hovered over her begonias and geraniums in the east window. They were always more luxuriant than those of others. She had one geranium called Madame Pollack that she often clipped and rooted for friends and relatives. It had the colors of sunset and autumn intermingled in its leaves. But few people besides mother could ever grow it.

However, the queen of her winter garden was a calla lily. All summer it kept aloof, resting up for its single midwinter blossom. Day after day during the cold weather mother watched the flower slowly unfold, and when finally it came into bloom, it was her pride and joy. She turned it back and forth, this way and that, and hung over it like a devoted acolyte.

It seemed the twisting of fate that so often this cherished blossom was offered up on the altar of her neighborliness. But so it was. Time and again there was a knock at the back door.

"Did ya hear, Mary? Ay-uh. The MacDougal girl went last night. Ay-uh. It's hard findin geranium leaves. So many froze that last storm. Her mother's all froze, too. I s'pose she was too worried and forgot ta cover em. But we heard yer calla was in bloom."

Anyone who's lived in the back country knows the sorrow of a coffin lowered to a winter grave without a single flower or bit of green. Many times all that could be managed was a wreath of geranium leaves. The house plants of the neighborhood would be culled till every geranium for miles around looked like it, too, was in mourning.

And so often when the calla was in bloom, a neighbor would wade through the snow and knock at the back door. Mother never refused, though she looked longingly as she cut and wrapped the blossom. Time and again the best of her winter garden was sacri-ficed to soothe someone else's dark time.

"Edna! Edna! . . . Yes, dear. Please bring up a pan of apples. Oh, and some cider, too. Hurry up now! Company's comin."

They were sour, tart apples, peeled, quartered, and dried on a rack in the oven. To make a pie mother soaked and cooked about two cups of them, adding sugar and a spoonful of boiled cider. Nutmeg and cinnamon were the seasoning. She spread a heavy cloth, floured it, and rolled out the dough. The undercrust was pinched high up around the pan. She spooned in the apples with a liberal hand, folded in a beaten egg, criss-crossed the top with dough, and baked. It came to the table like a queen in golden tiara, still warm, the latticework brushed with maple syrup. And on state occasions it was heaped with a snowdrift of meringue.

How she could cook! She knew to a dot how much soda was needed for milk so many days old. And those sour cream biscuits of hers! I tried for two years to teach a French-trained chef how to make mother's chicken pie, but it always failed.

Mother gloried in her family. She believed in us, and she helped us believe in ourselves. And she lived on wings. There was always something in her welcome— and always backed up by a full cookie jar or flaky biscuits or flapjacks and maple syrup. My cousins loved to pay her a visit. And all of us missed her dearly when the day came that her eager, shining face no longer gazed at us from the window.

THE ANIMULES

Location: told at Cranberry Lake, St. Lawrence County, c. 1900
Source: Albert Vann Fowler, ed., *Cranberry Lake 1845-1959*
(1959) Copyright © 1959 by the Adirondack Museum. Retold by
permission.
Of the old-time guides whose tall tales come down to us, Willard
Howland, who told these tales, had the most fanciful imagination.
Also from Howland: "The Scree," 129

Wal, I wahnt scairt fer myself. I can git away from them animules. But I dassent let you gals git mixed up with em. They's always takin after young gals.

"But Willard, you said swamp augurs can't run."

No, Miss Kitturithy, they can't run. But . . . they can slither. An they's mighty ugly critters. Specially if'n there's a wooly nig near.

Looked ta me like one of em was borin a nest fer hisself in that hackmatack stump. Fact, I was scairt long that piece a corduroy. I calated on gittin you gals out a there soon's I could.

"Oh, you're just trying to scare us!"

Oh, ya think so, do ya? Wal, it's true they aint got no legs. But they's nigh as fast as a snake. An ya gotta watch out fer that snout a theirn. Built all curly-que like a augur. They can bore right through a log with that nose. I seen em smash a boat ta smithereens.

"You saw a wooly nig?"

Wal, I knew he was hidin.

"How?"

Cause a them three-toed tracks a hissn—up on that high bank we come to north a the swale. Ya know that ironwood stick I was tottin? Wal, I was all set ta clobber one of em if'n I seen him stick his hairy snout out a the bushes.

"But why didn't you show us the tracks?"

Cause you'd a ben twice as scairt is why. Jest think if one a them critters come out a his hole an took after ya. That's why I wouldn't let ya go up that hill. They was wooly nig tracks all over. And a gouger's, too! It was lucky I got you gals out a there. Mebby it don sound right, Miss Kitturithy. Course, thanks ta me you aint never had a wooly nig chasin after ya up a steep grade. I didn't tell ya but his hind legs is twice as long as his front-ons. That way he don slip down backards. But he can make it purty hot for ya on the up-grade.

He lives most a his life on a hill, a-runnin up an a-backin down—so's he can git a fresh start. No, it's true! Ask any a the old-timers round here. They'll tell ya. I aint stringin ya. They's seen a lot a young gals git chased by them critters. An when ya got a wooly nig an a sidehill gouger on the same moun'n, wal! that's when a gal like you don have much of a chance nohow.

"A gouger?"

Yes, ma'm. But ya don see many a them. Mebby one er two a year. Lumberin's scairt most of em off.

"Are they big?"

Wal, depends. Ya see, a gouger's got legs on one side longer'n on t'other. Lady gougers got short legs on the right, and boy gougers, they got em on the left.

Now what they do is, they spend most a their time on a hill goin round an round an round. Course they don go the same way. The lady gouger, she goes this way, and her boy-friend, he comes long this way. An then, oh, once er twice a week, they git tagether . . . fer supper. Leanin agin one-nother.

If'n one of em gits bored and wants ta see what's happenin on nother moun'n, he has ta drag hisself ta git there. An that scrapes the hair off, so they don like ta do it.

But like I saw, lumberin's kilt most of em off. Them lumberjack's start cuttin a hill down the bottom, workin their way up. Drivin the gouger round an round ahead of em. Course bein drove round like that there aint no time fer supper. So he's gettin purty wobbly. Then when he gits up top, ya see him standin sidewise of a cliff. Like they's kinda confused. Cause there aint no place else ta go. An that's when the lumberjack comes along an knocks em off.

They's most as big as a buck. Big horns on em.

"Don't they chase boys?"

No, No. If'n they see ya got pants on, they jest look t'other way. Course if they aint seen womenfolks fer a long time, they might take after a boy. But it's young gals they like the best. An the prettier they is, the better they like em. A gal like you'd have a deuce of a time with a wooly nig.

An I'll tell ya somethin else. Cause where they's a wooly nig, they's most likely a side-windin gouger. An if'n ya git away from them two, they's genrally a swamp augur waitin fer ya down the bottom.

"Willard, have you ever seen a bear?"

Wal now, come ta think of it, I aint seen a bear fer a couple year now. But ya never can tell. We might see one tamarra.

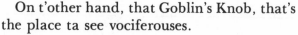

On t'other hand, that Goblin's Knob, that's the place ta see vociferouses.

"What?"

Vociferous. Vociferous antismasses. Yes'm. They's ones grabs womenfolks by the hair and yanks em up in the trees.

"Why do they do that?"

Ta hang ya there. Then they cut yer hair off an let ya drop. They chomp through with them long teeth a theirn. Oh, they's real greedy fer hair. Like ta have it round ta chaw on. An yeller hair like yers is what they like best. Makes no odds what happens ta the head.

"That's all they do?"

Yes'm. They jest tie yer hair round a tree till it comes loose — or they chaw it off. Oh now, don git me wrong. They jest like womenfolk's hair. Lot a the stuff gits lost up here.

"What's it look like?"

Wal, they's a whole lot a differnt kinds. They's the antis-smasses kind, an the antis-dorrus kind, an — But all of em, they got seventeen legs.

"What?"

Yes'm. Eleven in front an . . . six in the rear. An a little stump tail. Now ya take a place where the trail runs under some thick spruce. Lot a deadwood jest over yer head? That's the sort a place they like like ta hide out.

They hang down by one a them hind legs, jest out a sight, till some womenfolks comes by. Ya know how womenfolks talks a lot? Bout dishes'n'wallpaper'n'stuff? Wal, that's what genrally wakes em up an gits their legs a-wigglin.

I knowed em reach down, knock my hat off. But he was jest lookin ta see if I was a boy er a girl. They can't see so good hangin upside down in that deadwood.

"Don't boys get their hair pulled?"

Oh, sometimes. If'n he's got long enough hair. But a seventeen-legger can't genrally grab holt a short hair. If'n I think they's a antis-dorrus up there, I pull my hat off, let em see. An I keep real quiet.

"Willard, tell about the whirlin whampus."

Oh, Miss Kitturithy! I wouldn't wanna scare you like that! Yer folks wan you ta sleep good tanight. An you'd have nuthin but nightmares.

· No, I think it's time fer you ta go inside an git some sleep . . . Now, now! Like you promised. Cause don ferget, we're goin to Goblin's Knob tamarra.

HOW I GOT A BEAR

Location: Keene Valley, Essex County, 1870s
Source: Charles Dudley Warner, *In the Wilderness* (1876)
Also from Warner: "A-Hunting of the Deer," 105; "Old Mountain Phelps," 65

There's always a good deal of discussion about bears—a general wish to see one and much speculation about what you'd do if you met one in the woods. But bears are scarce and timid, and they reveal themselves only to a favored few. My own encounter was unpremeditated on both sides. I wasn't looking for a bear, and I have no reason to suppose a bear was looking for me. The plain truth is we were both out picking berries and we met by chance.

It was a warm, lazy August afternoon, the sort of day you want to sit and read something. But it occurred to the housekeepers in our cottage—of which there were four—it occurred to them to send me up the mountain to pick blackberries. They were up there that very morning. They couldn't believe their eyes—berries everywhere and all going to waste. We have a series of clearings that run up the mountain, much overgrown with bushes and briers. Cows pasture there, meandering in their sober fashion through the leafy passages as they browse among the bushes. I was furnished with a six-quart pail and told not to be gone long. A pie crust was already in the making.

To save appearances I also took a gun. It adds to the manly aspect of a person with a tin pail if he also has a gun. It was a Sharpe's carrying a ball cartridge, ten to the pound. It belonged to a friend of mine who wanted to shoot deer with it. He could hit a tree every time. That is, if the tree were of a good size, and the wind wasn't blowing, and the atmosphere was just right, and the tree wasn't too far off. But somehow the deer he fired at always got away.

I should add that I myself am no sportsman. Once, many years ago, I did shoot a robin in a cherry tree. I loaded my father's shotgun, crept up under the tree, and rested the muzzle on a fence about ten feet from the bird. I shut both eyes and pulled the trigger. What I afterwards saw scattered about on the ground utterly disgusted me with the life of a sportsman. I mention this incident in order to show that although I went blackberrying armed, there wasn't much inequality between myself and any creatures I might encounter.

I should also add that bears had occasionally been seen in these blackberry patches. One summer our cook was up there with a little girl from the neighborhood when a bear came out of the woods and walked happily towards them. The girl took to her heels and escaped, but poor Aunt Chloe was paralyzed with terror. She sat down where she was and began to weep and scream.

This seemed to bewilder the bear. He approached and looked at her. He walked round and surveyed her. Apparently he'd never seen a cook behave like this and he couldn't decide if she'd be good to eat. At any rate, after watching her a while, he turned around and went back to the woods. That's an authentic instance of the delicate feelings of bears.

When I'd climbed halfway up the hill, I set the rifle against a tree and began picking. Lured on from bush to bush by the gleam of fruit—which always promises more in the distance than when you reach it—I climbed farther and farther up the mountain. I heard bells clinking, twigs snap, and the stamping of cattle as they shook off the flies. Occasionally I encountered a cow flecked with sunlight, jowls a-chewing. It would gaze at me a moment then saunter off. I grew accustomed to this quaint society and attributed all the noises I heard to the cattle.

Blackberrying on a warm afternoon is dreamy work, and somehow my mind wandered onto bears. I was thinking up a magazine story I might write. Nothing special. Just something for one of the family magazines. It was about a she-bear who lost her cub and seized a little girl to replace it. The kidnapping would occur right here in this wood—of course! while her mother was picking blackberries. I made note of the wildflowers the little girl would be playing with when it happened.

The bear would carry her up to a cave in the mountain and raise her on milk and honey. When she was old enough to run away, she would escape. I hadn't determined yet how her father would recognize her after so many years, but he would. (As I say, it was only a magazine story.) And when his daughter told him about the bear—There's another problem: Who taught her English? For most of the school term she'd have been fast asleep in the arms of her foster mother.

Anyway, when his daughter tells her father about the bear, he becomes most indignant. He goes up the mountain and shoots the bear. And the bear, with her dying breath, turns reproachful eyes upon her murderer. The moral would have something to do with love and motherhood and kindness to animals.

As I was mulling over this tale I happened to look up . . . and see a bear. She was standing at the other end of the clearing and doing the same thing I was doing—picking berries. With one paw she bent down the bush, and with the other she clawed all the berries she could into her mouth. She made no distinction at all between green and ripe. Then all of a sudden she stopped eating berries. She dropped down and regarded me with a glad surprise.

It's all very well and good to speculate what you'd do under such circumstances, but I'll wager you wouldn't do it. My first thought was to climb a tree. But that's ridiculous with such a good climber behind you. If I ran away, I was sure she'd give chase. And although it's rumored a bear can't run downhill as fast as it can run uphill, nevertheless I was pretty sure she could get through these briers faster than I could.

The bear was approaching as these thoughts raced through my head.

Then I thought of a way I might divert her attention till I got back to the rifle. My pail was nearly full of berries, much better berries than the bear could pick for herself. So I set the pail on the ground and backed off, keeping one eye firmly on the beast—as lion tamers do.

And it worked. The bear went up to the berries and stopped. Not accustomed to eating out of a pail, she knocked it over and nosed about in the fruit, snuffling it up like a pig, all mixed with leaves and dirt. As soon as her head was down, I turned and ran.

Actually, a bear is much worse than a pig. Whenever they raid a maple sugar camp in the spring, they invariably upset all the buckets, trampling about in the sticky mess and wasting much more than they eat.

Somewhat shaky and out of breath, I reached the rifle. It wasn't a moment too soon. Enraged at my duplicity, the bear came crashing through the brush.

I felt the time of one of us was probably short, so I made a hasty review of my life. Do you know how hard it is to think of any good things you've done? The sins come out uncommonly strong. All I could remember was a newspaper subscription I delayed paying until both the paper and the editor were dead.

The bear was getting closer. I cocked the gun.

I tried to remember what I'd read about encounters with bears. I could think of plenty of times when a bear had run away from a man. But I couldn't think of a single instance when a man had escaped from a bear.

She was getting still closer.

I tried to think what the best way is to shoot a bear. Should I aim for the head and try to plant the ball between the eyes? No. That's too risky. A bear's brain is rather small, and if you miss that, it doesn't seem to mind a bullet or two in the head.

What about a bullet planted just back of the foreleg and sent to the heart? Death would follow instantly. But that's a hard spot to reach—unless the bear stands still and holds its side up to you.

Should I fire lying on my stomach? Or lying on my back with the gun resting on my toes?

By now I judged she could see the whites of my eyes.

I fixed my last thoughts on my family. My family's small, so this was not difficult. Dread of displeasing my wife was uppermost in my mind. What would be her anxiety for the pie as hour after hour went by and no blackberries arrived? And what would she say when the news came that her husband had been eaten?

What would they put on my tombstone?

Here lie the remains
of Charles D. Warner
Eaten
on August 20th, 1875

Finally I raised the gun and let go. Then I ran.

Not hearing the bear in pursuit, I looked back. She was lying in the grass. There was a quiver in her hind leg.

I remembered the best thing to do after firing a rifle is reload it, which I did, keeping one eye on the bear. She didn't move. Was she play-acting? Bears love to do that. It did seem, though, that her end had come and with merciful suddenness. I crept back. She was calm in her apparent death. That she might remain so into eternity, I blew out her brains and ran for home.

Notwithstanding my excitement, I managed to enter the kitchen with an unconcerned air.

"Charles, where have you been? And where's your pail?"

"I left it."

"You left it? But why?"

"A bear wanted it."

"Charles. Stop clowning! The pie crust is ready."

"Well, the last time I saw the pail a bear had it."

"Oh come now! Charles? You didn't really see a bear, did you?"

"Yes I did."

"What happened? Are you all right? Did he run?"

"Yes."

"Where?"

"After me."

"Charles! I don't believe a word of this. Well, what did you do?"

"I shot it."

"Charles!"

"Well, if you don't believe me, go up the mountain and look. It was too big to bring down alone."

Eventually I convinced the household something had occurred. Then I went down to the valley for help. The chief bear hunter of the region runs a boarding house there. He received my tale with a smile and a nod, as did his boarders. However, as I insisted and offered to lead them to the scene, a party of forty or fifty started out to bring in the bear.

All the way up the mountain they scoffed and jeered. Nobody believed there was a bear. But everyone who could find a gun carried it along. And the rest went armed with pitchforks and sticks. When finally I pointed to where the bear lay, a wooley mound in the grass, something like shock seized them all. They drew together, and silently they crept up round the beast, wide-eyed with wonder.

They made quite a show as they carried my prize into the village. Our best preacher never drew such a crowd. They said it was small for a bear, but Mr. Deane pronounced it a fair shot.

And that night, as bears and lions and alligators chased across the bedroom ceiling, my last delicious thought was, "By jove, Charles! You got a bear!"

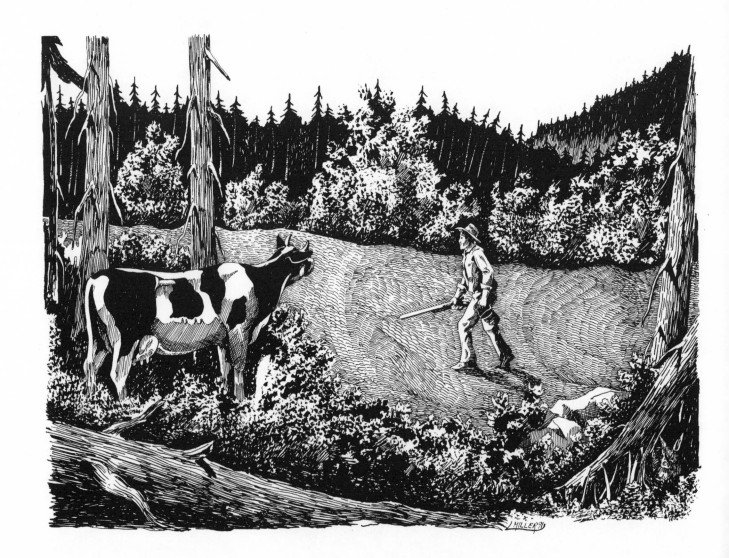

THE SCREE

Location: told at Cranberry Lake, St. Lawrence County, 1890s

Source: Albert Vann Fowler, ed., *Cranberry Lake 1845-1959* (1959). Copyright © 1959 by the Adirondack Museum. Retold by permission.

Willard Howland, a Cranberry Lake guide, invented this unique melding of the ghost story and the tall tale.

Also from Howland: "The Animules," 117

I was pokin long the draw till I come on a good spot fer settin traps. Pulled the boat up.

You 'member they drawed the water way down. It come off so dry them stumps up Dead Crick was three foot out the water. Cap a snow top each one, an I was glad a that!

Wal, I must a gone in a fur piece, cause next thing I knowed it come dark. So I climbed back where I left the boat. But there wahnt no sight of it.

I hunted fer that cussed boat a half hour. But twahnt no use. Never did find out what ailed it. But next day I seen it floating down in the floodwood. They was devilment loose! An damn if I didn't leave my coat'n that boat.

Wal, there wahnt no gettin home. Less'n I grew wings an flew. Trouble was, the only shack close by was Mossy Cobble's, an that's half way round the Hawk's Nest a

couple mile. It was sleepin in the snow tryin ta keep a fire goin, else walk them two mile through waterlogs an stumps.

The dark let down on them drowned woods black as a pocket. I calated I better leg it round ta Mossy's.

So I follered the old crick bed. But couldn't see half a rod ahead a me. If it wahnt fer that huntin snow layin long the draw, showin up the roots'n'sogs, I'd a had a deuce of a time.

Then a root grabbed holt a my boot, an I seen somethin white scootin the water. Bout a rod ahead. Scootin the water. First I thought it was snow. Didn't pay it no mind. But then somethin brushed my face, somethin wet an quick-like. First I says mebby it's one a them "white bats" I hear tell of. Then I says no, it's too cold fer bats.

I went on a piece an was holdin to a stump, tryin ta git over a big pine log. Somethin pushed me. An a seven-foot scree whooshed outta that stump. I was up next him. Poked my fist clean through his white belly. An when I drawed it out, they was a big hole.

I swan ta goodness!

An that scree did his cussed worst ta keep me from gettin ta Mossy's. He git down them holler stumps where the hi-hoes nest. An when I come to it, up he whooshed outta there like a sky rocket. Rizzed every hair on my head.

Next I seen his grinnin white skull poke out a rotten stump. Right front a my nose. An come the third time he done it, that's when I knowed who it was. The one knifed a squaw back in the old days. 'Member? We found him? Stuck in the mud, up ta his neck, his eyes wide open? I tell ya, the cold sweat an the gooseflesh come out.

I was mebby halfway ta Mossy's. An it was git there er freeze. Cause I was too tired ta stay awake an keep a fire goin.

That killer scree took ta lyin ahind a big log I have ta climb over. An jest as I get to it, he'd reach out them long hands an try ta grab me. Course he didn't have strength, cause he wahnt made out a nuthin but frog spit. But jest ta see him whooshin out made ya pretty nigh lose yer balance all to itself.

Couple time he pushed me flat over. Then he knocked my hat off an run them frog hands back a my ears.

Got so I was scared a ever piece a floodwood I come to. I thought the snow under my feet'd jump up an grab me. My hat was gone. I was covered with that stinkin bottom mud. An him grabbin my boots.

Must a cracked my shins forty-eleven time on them scree logs. I bet half the snags a the whole drowned land was blowed up the Hawk's Nest that night.

Wal, come the last bend, there by Mossy's Rock. It's jest a few rod from Mossy's landin. I says ta myself, I know that bottom. I'll run the rest. But twahnt long afore that screechin scree threw a stump. An it blame near cracked my head open.

My tongue was hangin out bout a foot comin up the path. The moon was hangin in them trees bright yeller. I made straight fer Mossy's door. Pantin like a whampus. An there, leanin agin it with his arms stretched out, was that seventeen-foot grinnin scree.

By gol! Two mile fightin the floodwood, an I gotta freeze ta death front a Mossy's door. Else let that scree inside an try ta sleep with it whooshin aroun.

I pulled at him. But there aint nuthin ta git aholt of in a man made out a frog spit. Then I seen somethin.

You know Mossy Cobble. He aint never ben right in the head. An when he built that shack, he screwed the door hinges ta the outside. Yah. So the door opens out-ways stead a inways.

Wal, I poked through that mess a frog spit an pulled the door open. An fore he can turn aroun, I'm inside an the door's shut. By dog! He put up a howl. I seen his fingers comin through the cracks. I had ta wire that door ta keep him out.

I tell ya, if that door wahnt hinged wrong end to, I wouldn't be here doin no talkin bout it.

THE OLD CHURCH

Location: Johnsburg, Warren County, 1860s

Source: Jeanne Robert Foster, *Adirondack Portraits* (1986). Copyright © 1986 by Noel Riedinger-Johnson. Retold by permission of Syracuse University Press.

New Year's Day, 1863, was when the Emancipation Proclamation took effect.

Also from Foster: "The Last Tarrin'n'Featherin," 85; "The Lumberjack's Tale," 49; "Nance's Baby," 35; "Sonny's Coat," 71

U p on the Putnam farm was a red house. "York brown" we called it. The paint was outcrop. Ya went up on Crane Mountain an got a bucket er two a red dirt. An when ya mixed it with oil, ya got York brown. Sort a reddish. An it lasted ferever.

Wal, jest east a that red house was a log cabin. It's where the preacher lived when he built the church. It was only logs, but it had a deep cellar. That's where Enos hid slaves, an at night he took em ta the next Underground. He had a stove down there ta keep em warm if they run away in winter.

He was one a the old Putnam breed, Enos Putnam.

His wife come from down below. She was a schoolteacher, a smart schoolteacher. An Enos, he was jest a farmboy. He couldn't read er write. But he fell in love. An he got the town clerk ta write his love letters. An after a time they got married.

First thing she done was, she taught him ta read'n'write. Then she said, "You shall be a preacher." An he was. After a time she got him ordained.

He built that church up at the crossroads. It's nigh ready ta fall down now, but one time it had a steeple and horse sheds. An after he done all that, some folks cat-called him at town meetin. They called Enos Putnam a nigger preacher.

Wal, the war come on, like Enos Putnam said it would. They fired on Fort Sumter. An the preacher's boy, Henry, he volunteered. He used ta write home bout the the boys singin in the trenches.

Then the preacher held a meetin. It was New Year's 1863. Folks helped him bore holes in boards so's he could set candles in the long winders. An that church blazed!

Enos read em the Declaration a Independence: "We hold these truths to be self-evident, that all men are created equal . . . " An he read Abe Lincoln's words that freed the slaves that day an fer ever'n'ever.

An while he was readin, a man opened the door and run up the aisle with a paper.

"It's fer the preacher," he said. An the preacher took it an opened it.

His hans shook, but he read it out loud. "We inform you . . . that your son . . . Henry Putnam . . . was killed . . . " The tears run down his cheeks, but he held out his hans and he said, "The

Lord giveth . . . an the Lord taketh away."

It's all quiet now round the old church. The preacher an his sons an his grandsons all sleep there. An Sybil, who taught him ta read an made him a preacher. The stones're leanin over. Some of em're sinkin down. They'll be covered soon. I s'pose folks won't remember . . .

You can go in. The door aint locked.

LETTER FROM PEA SOUP LAKE

Location: Essex County, 1940s

Source: Harry M. MacDougal, *Pete Pequoix of Pea Soup Lake* (1949) Copyright © 1949 by Harry M. MacDougal and John B. Tefft. Retold by permission of Helen MacDougal Richards.

For thirty-three years Harry MacDougal (1883-1972) was Essex County Clerk. His stories of Pete Pequoix of "Pea Soup Lake" made him a popular after-dinner speaker. A lifelong Republican, he often used these occasions to poke fun at Democrats. During World War II he began writing about Pete's adventures in the form of letters to *The Ticonderoga Sentinel*.

Further reading: Carlin O. Walker, "Remembering Harry Mac-Dougal," *The Valley News* (Elizabethtown, 21 Sept. 1988)

Pea Soup Lake
Froze

Deer Jackunbill,
Dis wedder! If it don kill me I tink I die. Rosie put fire in de stove an de smoke freezed in de pipe. I have go up top de house taw it out. An when I come down — Rosie! she take de latter bout ten minute before.
Rosie no good for smart. But she awful good for stout. She break de scale at 17 an 400 pound. She chop 2 cord wood on de day. An she hoe de potato. Me I do de

heavy ting. Like keep eye in de stove when she cook. I have watch her, tink up job. If I don watch, Rosie step on de cow an kill heem.

Udder day I see Rosie look trew de window. I am in de wood count de crow. De boy from Washington come. He ask how many animal you have? We have de cow. An we have de crow. Sometime dey is 2 hundert. Udder day probly million. Dey use come de fall, go home de spring. Now dey come when dey feel like, go home when it please. You ask me dis one dem Rosiewelt "New Deal."

Rosie don count. So I out in de wood. I see her look trew de window. I holler brang de cider! But she shake de head, keep on de look. "Brang de cider!" An she shake de head an keep look. So I am mad. I go in dar. Bahgosh. It was de houn dog. Bot of dem, de cheek fall down.

Dos boy in Washington. Where dey go school?

Rosie get lettair from de Big Boss—Rosiewelt. He have big farm. He tell Rosie put de ceiling on de blueberry. Rosie say he don know blueberry. He mus trink cider when he write dat. He mean put de blueberry on de ceiling. Den he say dirty-five cent on de quart.

Rosie tink bout dat. She go in de outdoor batroom an she tink bout dat. Mr. Gonyear he pay 15 cent on de quart. Rosie think bout dat. Den she make up de mine, now on she pick por de Big Boss. An he can have all de blueberry he wan. She make me put big hole in de ceiling. An she hang de blueberry. An wat you tink? Dat Big Boss Rosiewelt he don come por de blueberry. Dey all go rot. Rosie say if dos boy in Washington wan blueberry dey just come pick it demself.

Den de Washington tole it you mus have blackout. Dey say blow out de lamp 9 on de clock. Don dos boy know? Dat late everybuddy is sleep.

Rosie is worrie. She ask wad we do? I have brain. I tole it, you set de larm. Den you wake up. You put fire in de lamp. An you blow it. An by dat you don compete wid de law.

But Mr. Gonyear don like. He tell Rosie don do dat. De Washington say rang de firebell. But Pea Soup don have her firebell.

So Joe LaRue he tink up a ting. He say dis de bes ding. Pete Donda live end de road.

Joe LaRue himself he live udder en. Mr. Gonyear he live halfway de middle on top his store. Joe say it, when de black come me an Pete Donda we bod take de cow out de barn. We put bell roun de cow neck. Mr. Gonyear run himself bot en de road. He say fire! fire! loud he can. When we hear Mr. Gonyear we hit de cow. By dat she run an rang de bell bod en de road.

Everybuddy tink dat ok. Cept Bill Anjon. He say he don hear cowbell. He live in de wood. So Mr. Gonyear give him her cowbell an tole it rang it an woke up herself. But Rosie don hear de bell. She don wake up. She don put fire on de lamp. You ask me it look like de jail por Rosie.

Mr. Gonyear say he run himself on de road. He call fire! fire! hit de cow! So Joe LaRue smack her cow. By dat she jomp an rang de bell. Loud she can.

Den she see Mr. Gonyear. An she run on Mr. Gonyear. He run himself fas he can back his store. But she don stop halfway. She keep on de run with Joe hole de rope. She run up war Pete Donda is wit her cow.

But Pete Donda cow don run. She stan. She don rang de bell. So Joe say kick de cow. Den Pete jomp on de back an kick de cow. Dat make her jomp! She rang de bell. Wit Pete on de back en hole on all he can.

Dat scare Joe LaRue cow. She turn roun rang her bell loud she can. She take Joe on de run back Mr. Gonyear store. But Joe foot twis an he lose de rope.

Den Pete Donda cow come wid Pete on de back en. He call stop de cow! So Mr. Gonyear he trow stone. Dat make de cow mad like Rosie. She trow Pete an break it her nose. Mr. Gonyear say when Pete nose is fix he break it back.

After dat I make up wit Rosie. She have bad time. She shave herself and cut it off her chin. She shave pass de glass. It don make big difference. She have 2 more chin.

But I make up. I give Rosie 2 grain bag wid big flower on it. I give her an tole is new dress. Mr. Gonyear say I can have. But firs I have promise—2 week don go close de cracker barrel. I say I promise an he give de bag. An I give it Rosie for new dress. It have big flower. All she have do is sew de bag. But Rosie don sew. But she fine some nail an she poun de dress. An when she take off she pull

out de nail. An if dos Germs an Japansers come bomb de house, dey not see ting. Dey tink she is big flower. An den Rosie can run hit wid her hoe.

You come see Little Pete. He have big brane. His hair so tick he look like wood-chuck. Dey don lie down his hair. Den Rosie put on it de pine tar. Now dey lie down but de fly come.

But he have big brane. De school, dey don put him back atall. 2 year now he stay right up in de turd grade. I teach him how spell. But de school don spell like me an he don get his grade.

Oh utter night we have big trouble. Bout halfway trew de house is jomp op down op down. Firs I tink it mus be Rosie. When she fix de breakfas de house always it jomp op down op down.

But den Rosie holler alert! alert! De Germs an Japan-sers! An a big jomp trow me out. An jus quick anudder jomp trow me back. Rosie holler dey bomb de house.

She run outdoor. She holler alert! alert! Den she holler all same ding she say when she hit me las Christmas. So loud she can she holler. De 4 and 10 kid dey jomp trew de window. Rosie fine her hoe. She say I get dem Germs and Japansers. I tole it good ding Rosie. You go der. I keep eye on de potato. Den Mr. Gonyear come. He say shut de mout. We have eart quake.

I have go feed de crow. Hope you are de same.

Respecful,
Pete Pequoix

PHANTOM FALLS

for Elizabeth Folwell and Tom Warrington

Source: William H. H. ("Adirondack") Murray, *Adventures in the Wilderness; or, Camp-Life in the Adirondacks* (1869)
There are no rapids and waterfalls in the Adirondacks like the ones described in this story. However, the legend of the Indian maiden is associated with two sites: Raquette Falls on the Raquette River, Franklin County, and Buttermilk Falls at the inlet to Long Lake, Hamilton County.
Also from Murray: "Crossing the Carry," 25; "Farewell to John Plumley," 149

Day after day we pushed our narrow cedar shell up one unexplored creek after another. For weeks we had not seen a human face nor heard a human voice other than our own. Our fire each night was built on the shore of some lake or pond which lay as it had for hundreds, even thousands of years, and where it is doubtful if fire was ever kindled before.

After hours of struggle our boat burst through a mass of alder bushes onto a sheet of water. It was framed by mountains and bordered here with grass and there with sand, and again with lilies whose fragrance in the late afternoon mingled with the scent of balsam and pine.

"John, let's make camp. I can scarcely unhook my fingers from the paddle!"

"I've made camp here before, Mr. Murray. Wouldn't mind seein the old place again. Fact is, somethin happened down by them hemlocks that still puzzles me."

As we proceeded down the lake the roar of a rapids came to our ears. Rover looked about excitedly, and as the shores converged, the boat began to sway in the action of the water. "Look at that white pine, will ya. I thought he wouldn't last another winter."

The tree stood like an angry sentinel, guarding a projection of land on the other side of which the rapids began. John gave a few sharp strokes which sent our boat up on the beach. Rover bounded toward the underbrush as we stepped ashore.

John insists he cooked twenty-one fish that night. Perhaps he did. We hadn't eaten since breakfast. Afterwards we threw some logs on the fire, lay down on our blankets, and gazed at the lake. The moon was just appearing above the eastern mountains, nearly at the full. A few of the larger stars struggled for attention, but soon even they paled beside the queen of the night as she rose and held her open court.

Now and then the trees along the western shore would rustle. Then the pines would feel the stir of airy fingers. And at length, when the zephyr reached the lake, the water, which an instant before had shone like seamless glass, would break in a thousand undulations.

"Mr. Murray, do you know we're camped on haunted ground?"

"Haunted?" I raised myself and looked in John's direction. "You don't believe in ghosts, do you?"

"Well, the trappers tell some mighty queer stories bout this place. An fifteen years ago this month I made camp here, an durin the night I saw somethin that wasn't human."

"Tell the story, John! It's a perfect night for ghosts."

"Fact is, Mr. Murray, I'd like ta know what ya think of it."

The woods were still as John filled his pipe and lit it from a splinter in the fire. Even the roar of the rapids seemed more to deepen than to dispel the quiet.

"Seems a branch a the Hurons hunted these shores. Their chief had a daughter named . . . Wisti. But the French called her Balsam cause her skin was dark.

"She fell in love with a priest. He come up from Canada ta convert the tribe. They used ta meet here in this cove. Finally he went back ta Montreal ta get released. He was gonna take the girl ta France with him. An they agreed ta meet here on a certain night in June.

"Well, the man never come back. He could a ben ambushed an killed, I s'pose. Or maybe he had second thoughts bout the girl. Anyways, ever night little Balsam brought her canoe round this point, an ever night she went home alone.

"She had other suitors. They come even from the big lakes. But she refused em all. She said her heart was in the north and wouldn't come back.

"So a year went by. An when the snow melted an the ice went out, little Balsam brought her canoe round here again. But the man was never here. Finally they say the light went out of her eyes. An one night when the leaves begun ta turn, she disappeared.

"Ever since, the trappers say somethin rises out a Phantom Falls down the bottom a them rapids. It's a canoe that leaves no wake. An in it there's a figure whiter than the snow."

"Well told, John!"

"It's true, Mr. Murray. I seen her."

"John?"

"Fifteen years ago this month. I was down the Black River, run my boat in here. The moon, the lake . . . was just about the way they are now.

"I went ta sleep—bout where yer lyin. Next thing I knew, my dog was rubbin his nose against me an whinin. I grabbed a rifle an looked about. We used ta have panthers up here. But not a twig snapped. I was gonna smack the dog when he run down by the lake.

"Comin round where them hemlocks are was a boat. It was a canoe with the ends curled up. There was a girl in it—or what looked like a girl. She had a paddle across her lap, an her head was turned—like she was listenin. She come right up here. Twice she looked me straight'n the eye. Then she shook her head an turned away. Only it didn't look ta me like her paddle ever really touched the water."

We sat a while in silence. At last John took a log which the fire had burned through the middle and turned the ends upon the coals.

"Mr. Murray? What ya think?"

"I don't know, John. I doubt you really saw what you think. Perhaps it's what the doctors call a mental delusion. You—"

Rover raised his head suddenly. A growl rumbled in his throat. He looked at John and lowered his head again.

"What probably happened was you—"

"Rover! Be quiet! Sorry, Mr. Murray."

"What probably happened was you were alone and tired. You'd been boating all day. You'd heard stories about this place. I—"

"Rover! Come back here! Mr. Murray! Look!"

I sprang to my feet. Something was approaching the camp. My rifle was in my hand without my knowing it.

It was a canoe—or what seemed to be a canoe. The figure in it was bent forward as if listening. It sat thus a moment then grew erect.

The face of a girl seemed imprinted within a white shroud round the head. The eyes were hollow, devoid of any reflection. They stared directly at me, and while they gazed I seemed unable to move. The clothing was just as John described it . . . only . . . it seemed to glow. Or perhaps it was the moonlight made it shine. I remember the moonlight fell across the prow of the boat as it projected from the shadow of the the trees.

It may have been a minute the apparition faced us. Then, with a shake of the head, it took the paddle and sank it in the water. But the paddle made no impression on the water, and not a ripple stirred as the boat turned and vanished round the point.

"Rover! Come here! Lie down! Well, Mr. Murray, what ya think now?"

"I'm not sure, John."

"Ya seen how that canoe was curved up at both ends? There aint any canoes like that round here. An that paddle—how thin it was."

"I saw, John, but . . . They didn't look real to me. And that face looked more like an outline than something solid."

"The Good Book says we'll all be changed at death, don't it?"

"Umm. John, I think I better sleep on that. Let's put some more logs on the fire."

We fed the fire, lingered a while in its cheery blaze, then wrapped ourselves in our blankets and lay side by side, our rifles close at hand, and Rover at our feet.

The sun was high before I woke. John was already making those twelve-inch pancakes of his. Surprisingly, my slumber had been deep and oblivious—the kind that takes the hours clean out of your life without even the filament of a dream by which the memory may connect the lying down and the rising up.

We cooked some trout from the day before, and a quart pan of coffee. Afterwards, having taken note of the weather—it was sparkling clear—we decided to explore the mystery of the ghost and mark out a course through the rapids towards which the phantom had disappeared.

"If she comes again tonight, John, we'll run alongside her and cut her off. Wadda ya say?"

"I say anythin you say, Mr. Murray."

So we launched the boat, and holding her in midstream, scanned the tremulous water below.

"Aim fer the center, Mr. Murray. The current'll take us. Looks ta me like the rocks up here're covered, so all we have ta do is dodge them two boulders. Now farther on there's some falls ta jump. An when ya hear the big roar, watch out! That's Phantom. It's twenty-five feet. More'n I care ta jump!"

"Agreed, John! Where do we land?"

"On the right, next a dead hemlock. It's about thirty rods upstream a the falls.

But we'll have ta jump her hard. The current's mighty strong there. Ya understand everythin?"

"Yes, John."

"All right then. Steady . . . Now!"

We lifted our paddles and glanced like an arrow down the watery slope. Down, down we drove, past rock and ledge, swerving this way and that, sweeping round boulders and overhanging pines.

"Don't worry bout the paddle, Mr. Murray. Smash it if ya have to!"

The current grew stronger and the flight swifter till we lifted on the brink of a falls and made a wild leap into the foam below. Up we bounced and floated on the pool.

Below us for some fifty rods lay a scene of turmoil and riot. The water slid over ledges or tore itself on rocks. Boulders lifted themselves on every hand.

"Keep ta the white water here!"

At the foot of the reach I could discern the rim of a falls. And farther on, shut off from view by a sharp curve, the plume of yet another falls rose upward.

Again we flew, and with a royal upleaping of blood took another jump. Onward round a curve, down another reach, over a third falls.

Fancy yourself leaping with us. We're heading towards a funnel through which, bursting, we must shoot a fourth falls. Its thunder rises above the crashing torrent.

We take the gorge, square in the center . . . And lo! the falls yawns beneath us! So you swing your paddle ahead and pull with all your might. The boat lifts, and for a second your heart leaps. Then down you plunge into a boiling caldron, and with another thrust dart up from beneath the seething mass.

Three times we ran the rapids. The most trying spot was at that hemlock, where we had to fight to escape the current. There the stroke of our paddles had to be as one and made with our united strength.

"So far, so good, Mr. Murray. Let's go down take a look at the big falls."

We forced our way through the underbrush, clambered down the bank, and stepped out on a shelf of rock. The falls presented a magnificent sight. They rose straight as a wall some twenty-five feet. The edge must have been notched or chipped, for spouts of water leaped upward, gathering rainbows in their feathery spray. The main rush of water could be seen behind this veil.

In one spot, though, the current flowed unimpeded. It was about eight feet across, near the middle. Here the water rolled over as smooth as glass.

"If ya ever get caught here, Mr. Murray, an have ta shoot these falls, aim fer the smooth patch. An put yer whole strength behind the paddle. Them rocks down there're mighty sharp. You'll have ta shoot past em or you'll get torn ta pieces."

"Lord, John! Maybe someone could do that, but not I! I'll wager not one man in fifty could shoot that distance."

"Ya never know where you'll find yerself when ya boat around as much as we do. Jest remember, steer fer the smooth water, an push off with all yer might."

"Is this where the Indian girl lost her life?"

"So they say. John Norton tells how he was camped down the bend one night. He says he saw somethin come out a the mist an go skimmin up the rapids. Poor John! He broke camp right then'n'there."

"I can well imagine. Maybe tonight we'll see if there's any truth in it."

It may have been eleven o'clock when we took our paddles, stepped into the boat, and pushed off. We glided toward the shadow of a hemlock. The silence was profound—as only the night can make it.

"John, this is the queerest ambush we've ever made."

"I was just thinkin the same, Mr. Murray. But ya know, I've wanted ta do this fer fifteen years. How ya feeling?"

"Oh, all right, but . . . John, I'd rather not run these rapids tonight. Moonlight isn't sunlight, and if you should make a mistake, or I—"

"Mr. Murray! When did you ever know John Plumley make a mistake in a boat? We've run rapids worse'n'these. Jest remember that dead hemlock an give a mighty push when you see it."

Here the conversation ceased, and we sat again in silence. Ten, twenty, thirty minutes passed. I began to feel impatient. I began to feel I was making a fool of myself. I took out my watch and held its face up to a beam of light coming down through the foliage.

Just then a low moan rose from our camp. Rover was outlined against the remains of the fire and trembling. He raised his head and sent forth that saddest of all sounds—the wailing cry of a hound. At the same instant I felt the boat shake.

"Mr. Murray, look."

Turning, I saw the phantom canoe. It was just rounding the point. The figure in it was bent forward as if listening. She held the paddle across her lap, yet the boat seemed guided in exactly the path I had witnessed the night before. It went straight up to the border of our camp.

The spectral arm rose slowly up and rested on the brow, as when one peers into darkness. Rover backed off, his tail between his legs. Then the arm sank upon the paddle again, and the boat turned of itself and glided away.

Out we shot from under our tree. The apparition turned round. We gave a stroke which bent our paddles like swords. Devil or saint we were upon her! I thrust out my hand . . . But I clutched only the empty air. She was twenty yards away and racing round the point.

We sent our boat flying. The bottom seemed to rest on the water rather than part it. The sides quivered from stem to stern.

Round the point we sped, pursuer and pursued. Then side by side into the current —and down over the verge. Into the rift, into the gloom of overhanging pines, out again into the moonlight.

We leaped the first cascade, and with hands and faces dripping, plunged down the second reach. Though we never missed a stroke, the phantom boat pulled ahead of us. The white face peered back. It showed an outline as though of flesh and blood. Yet when we sped through moonlight it seemed a thing transparent.

We gained on her again, and as we leaped a falls, in mid-air, I reached out my hand and closed it on her form. But I grasped only the atmosphere. No hand would ever touch her, or if it did, the human senses would be too gross to feel the contact.

Just then she rose to her feet and waved us back. The look on her face was almost plaintive. Her arms dropped as our boats sped between two boulders. Then she flung them high in a wild gesture and pointed downstream. The roar of Phantom Falls was upon us!

I tapped the side of the boat with my paddle and felt an answering shake from John. We swept round a curve. The hemlock came in sight. I seized my paddle and reached down the blade. But even as I bent to the stroke I heard a crack—and a cry from John. His paddle had snapped!

I threw the last ounce of my strength into that stroke, but the suction was too strong. It seized John's end of the boat and flung us back out into the current. We were tumbling towards the falls!

It is said the mind acts with supernatural quickness at times like these. I righted the boat, directed the bow downstream, and reached my paddle to John. Never shall I forget the look on his face. It was plain as speech. "All that man can do, Mr. Murray. All that man can do."

I watched him take two strokes, then turned in my seat and crouched low. How could he keep so steady? The motion was frightful. My face was contracted under the pressure of the wind.

We were heading straight for the middle. I grasped the rim of the boat on each side with either hand. Quicker and quicker the moment came. The boat trembled, then quivering like a frightened fish it gave a mighty leap and sprang out over the abyss.

Down we shot through the moonlit night. Practice had taught me how to hold the declination, and we struck the water like a stake. Instantly John and I sprang upward. By some miracle of strength he had shot us safely past the rocks.

We swam to the edge of the pool, and climbed out, and lay for a time, side by side, on a sloping ledge, in the shadow of the pines, while the violence of our hearts and lungs subsided.

We found our boat drifted ashore at the lower end of the pool—and John's broken paddle beside it. Shouldering the craft and striking eastward, we came to the carry, crossed it, reached the lake, and in five minutes more stood wringing our clothes beside the fire.

"John, I'm going to write an account of this."

"No one'll believe it, Mr. Murray."

"I don't care if they believe me. I'm going to write it. There's no doubt in my mind that you're standing in front of me this very moment, wringing the water out of your jacket. And there's no doubt about that broken paddle on the ground beside you. And we both know something more than human appeared off our camp two nights running. And you and I both know we took that boat of yours and chased it."

And so I've kept my promise and told the story. And now I'll leave it to each of you to decide for yourselves just how much or how little you see fit to believe.

FAREWELL TO JOHN PLUMLEY

Source: William H. H. ("Adirondack") Murray, "In Memoriam,"
Woods and Waters (summer 1901), 7-8
Also from Murray: "Crossing the Carry," 25; "Phantom Falls," 141

WILLIAM H. H. ("ADIRONDACK") MURRAY

They tell me he is dead . . .

What a foolish fashion of speech.

Not till the woods are destroyed to the last tree, not till the mountains have crumbled to their bases and the lakes dried up will that man be dead. For John Plumley was the woods. He was the mountains, the streams. He personified them.

It is twenty years now since I was last in those woods of which he taught me so much. Twenty years since he and I met and parted? If I stooped down and got very close to the ground, do you suppose I might even now be able to find the old trails we blazed out so long ago?

He taught me a faultless knowledge of the woods—the name and nature of plant and tree, the languages of the night. While I, blunderingly, expounded on the names of stars and planets and constellations and of the greater splendor beyond. But mostly, mostly he looked—and saw—or listened and heard but said nothing. For he possessed that sweetest of all gifts, the gift of silence.

All trails were blazed trails to him. He was the only guide I ever knew who never lost himself or his way.

You say he is dead? What a vulgar way to state a sublime fact. For I know I will meet John again. And not as an old man wearied by toil, but as John Plumley himself—strong and vigorous, at fullest prime. And he and I will journey again by sunlight and starlight as in the days of old.

John, do you remember the signal I used to give when coming up the river at twilight? When I, too, am borne down that last river, you will hear my call again as I seek the shore where you have made a quiet camp already. And there, as the years fall away, the fellowship of the woods will be ours again, this time forever and ever.

Happy meeting, John. Good cheer, old friend.

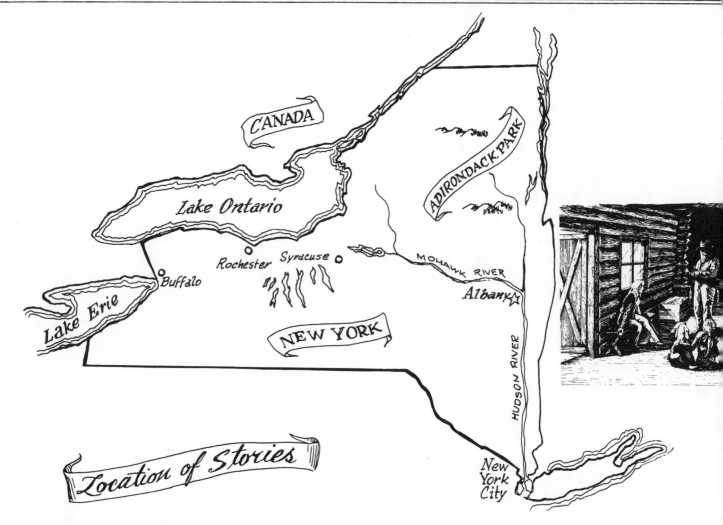

Map showing Lake Ontario, Lake Erie, Canada, Buffalo, Rochester, Syracuse, Mohawk River, Albany, Adirondack Park, Hudson River, New York, New York City

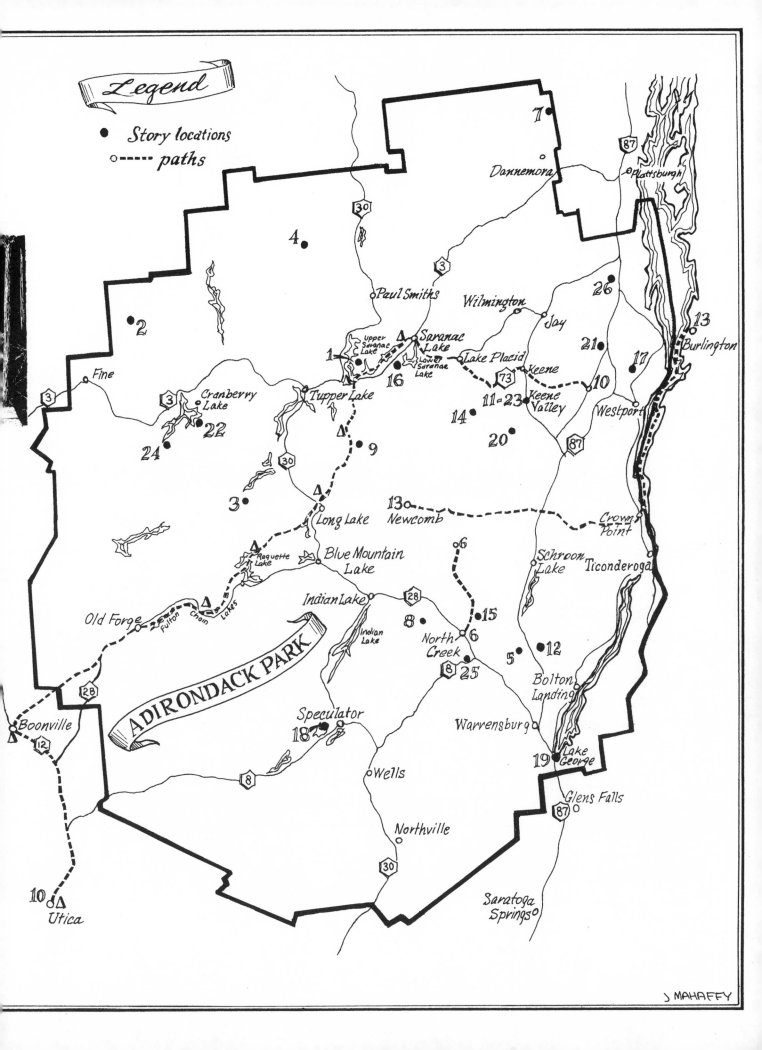

INDEX OF SOURCES BY AUTHOR